THE POWER OF NO DOUBT

THE POWER OF NO DOUBT

NICHOLAS DAVID

First Edition, First Printing: 2024
ISBN: 979-8-3481-6130-9
Cover Design by: Nicholas David
Interior Design by: Nicholas David

Published by **NO DOUBT Ink**
www.powerofnodoubt.com

For permissions, inquiries, or bulk orders, contact:
info@powerofnodoubt.com

Daniel Redd (Left) & Brother Nicholas David (right)

Dedication To my brother Daniel Redd, whose passing awakened in me the strength to transform pain into power, and whose memory continues to fuel my journey of growth and discovery. I love you and I miss you.

Contents

Preface

FROM ROCK BOTTOM TO UNWAVERING BELIEF

The phone slips from my fingers, my knees hit the carpet, and my world splits in two. My mom's voice echoes through the phone: "No one has seen your brother in two weeks."

November 23rd. My birthday. The day everything changed. But let me show you what happens when life breaks you open—not to destroy you, but to reveal what you're truly made of.

4:30 AM. Three months later.

I'm on my bedroom floor, muscles trembling, sweat dripping onto the carpet. Push-up number 491 out of 1,000. Each rep isn't just about physical strength anymore. Each one is a declaration: Pain doesn't get to break me. It gets to build me.

"Ten more, Nick. Just ten more," I tell myself, teeth gritted.

Another voice, darker and sharper, cuts in: *"What are you doing? Normal people don't do this."*

I push harder. "I'm not after normal... 492...493..."

My whole body shakes as I lower myself again. The burn in my chest rises, but so does my determination.

"Don't quit now. You've got this."

The doubt is back: *"Why even try? You'll just fail again. Isn't that your thing? Starting strong, then fizzling out?"*

I pause, forehead against the sweat-soaked carpet. "Not this time," I whisper. "Not anymore."

I made a declaration to myself and to the Universe, to God: "I will give my life for this change. I'm willing to do whatever it takes. I will not give up."

But let's rewind. Before the push-ups. Before this transformation.

Picture a young man in a cubicle, slouched at a desk, staring at yet another mundane used car advertisement on the computer screen. That was me, dying a slow death in the limbo between who I was and who I dreamed of being.

Have you ever felt it? That gnawing ache when you know you're built for more, but fear grips you tight? When every dream feels like a joke, a mirage just out of reach? I tried running from it—late nights, cheap thrills, empty laughter. Anything to drown the voice that reminded me I was wasting my potential. Depression didn't creep in; it stormed the gates and made itself at home.

In that moment, life gave me a choice: let the pain consume me or let it ignite me.

I chose fire.

This book isn't about push-ups or motivational slogans. It's about a relentless belief buried inside each of us, waiting to be set free.

It's about transforming from:

- A self-doubting dreamer to someone who builds a six-figure business
- A lost soul to someone who moves across the world during a global pandemic
- A person crushed by loss to someone who turns pain into rocket fuel

But more than that, it's about you. About who you could become when you strip away self-doubt and step into the power of NO DOUBT.

Inside these pages, we'll tackle what's holding you back, uncover the tools to build unshakeable momentum, and learn how to use your pain to propel you to places you never thought possible. This isn't a quick fix or a feel-good read. It's a battle-tested blueprint for turning fear into fuel and dreams into reality.

Whether you're:

- Stuck in a soul-draining job
- Paralyzed by the fear of failure
- Or someone who feels destined for more but just can't break through

This book is your wake-up call.

Those 1,000 push-ups? They're not about strength. They're about proving—every day—that you're capable of more than you ever believed. Maybe for you, it's writing that first page, launching that business, or simply standing up when life knocks you down.

Are you ready to rise before dawn, to meet fear with ferocity, and to claim the life waiting for you?

Let's get it.

How to Use This Book

This isn't just another book to read - it's a blueprint for transformation. Here's how to get the most out of it:

1. Read it Actively

Don't just highlight - take action. Each chapter ends with specific challenges and exercises. Do them. The magic isn't in knowing - it's in doing.

2. Start Where You Are

You don't need perfect conditions to begin. Whether you're in a dead-end job dreaming of more or already on your journey, these principles work if you work them.

3. Use the Framework

- Each chapter builds on the previous ones
- Key Takeaways summarize crucial lessons
- "Your Turn" sections provide immediate action steps

• Real-world examples show principles in action

4. Make It Personal

Take what resonates and make it your own. Your journey won't look exactly like mine or anyone else's. That's the point. Use these tools to unlock your unique power.

5. Revisit and Revise

Come back to different chapters as you need them. Some lessons will hit differently as you grow. Let this book be a living resource for your continuing evolution.

Remember: This book isn't about motivation - it's about transformation. Don't just read it. Live it.

Let's get it.

PART I: THE AWAKENING

Before you can build an empire, before you can change the world, before you can truly embrace the power of NO DOUBT, you must first wake up. This awakening rarely comes gently - it often arrives as a shock, a loss, a moment that splits your life into "before" and "after."

In these next three chapters, you'll witness my own awakening - through the raw pain of loss, the facade of external validation, and the journey to true self-knowledge. This isn't just my story though. It's a mirror for your own awakening, a chance to recognize the moments in your life calling you to something greater.

The awakening isn't comfortable. It's not meant to be. But it's necessary. Because you can't build a masterpiece on a foundation of sleep.

Let's begin.

1

The Foundation of Power: Know Thyself

"Knowing yourself is the beginning of all wisdom."
— *Aristotle*

The fluorescent light buzzes overhead like it's counting down the seconds of my life. It's 3:21 am and I'm standing in front of a dirty bathroom mirror, eyes bloodshot from another night masking insecurities in cheap beer and hollow laughter.

'Who are you, Nick?'

The question hits me like a sucker punch to the soul.
Not because it's profound. *But because in that moment I didn't have a damn answer.*

Have you ever stood there, really stood there, and looked yourself in the eye? Not the quick glance while brushing your teeth. Not the surface check before a date. I mean really look - past the mask, past the bullshit, past all the layers of who you think you're supposed to be?

Most people never do. Because what's staring back isn't just a reflection - it's a mirror to every lie you've ever told yourself. And let me tell you something: In that moment, with bass still thumping from the bar in my ears and another wasted night buzzing through my body, I saw every single one of those lies:

- The lie that I was "finding myself" when I was really hiding
- The lie that I was "living life" when I was really running from it
- The lie that I was "almost ready" when I was really just afraid

You know these lies. Maybe you're living them right now.

But here's the thing about 3 AM drunk mirror moments - they either break you or wake you. And something in me refused to break.

The Awakening

Think about a time you've been underwater too long. That moment when your lungs are burning, your vision going dark, and every cell in your body is screaming for air. That's what real self-discovery feels like.

Because here's what nobody tells you about finding yourself: You don't do it in comfort. You don't do it in safety. You do it in moments that feel like drowning, when everything you thought you knew about yourself gets stripped away.

I spent years being what everyone else wanted:

- The "nice" friend
- The agreeable employee
- The guy who never rocked the boat

But every role I played, every mask I wore, was just another brick in the wall between me and my truth.

The Four Pillars of Self-Knowledge

Through my journey from that bathroom mirror to where I am now, I discovered what I call the Four Pillars of Self-Knowledge. Not some philosophical theory - real, raw, life-in-your-face truth about who you are and what you're capable of.

1. Values: Your Inner Compass

Let me show you exactly when I understood what values really mean. I'm sitting in a work meeting, nodding along while my soul withered. "The ad numbers look good this month. Good job everyone..." But something in my chest feels like it's being crushed under the weight of every half smile, every "yea, sure" to more work that should've been a "hell no."

My bank account was barely being fed, and my spirit's getting weaker. Then it hits me - this isn't about the job. This isn't even about the money. This is about betrayal. Not of the company, not of the team (shout out to the awesome people there), but of something far more sacred: my own truth.

Here's what nobody tells you about values: They're not just fun words you put on your vision board. They're the hills you're willing to die on. The lines you refuse to cross. The truth that flows through your bones when everything else goes dark.

For years, I thought I valued success. Status. Recognition. Money. Power. But standing in my bathroom at 3 AM, success didn't mean shit. What I really valued was:

- Growth that changed me
- Truth that stripped me bare
- Impact that outlived me
- Creation that came from my soul

Now, Here is your first action step:
Right now, grab a pen. Write down everything you think you value. Then, next to each one, write down the last time you actually made a decision based on it.

2. Strengths: Your Hidden Power

Picture this: I'm fifteen, sitting in my high school guidance counselor's office. My dad's words echo in my head: "You don't want to end up a starving artist." I loved art, but instead, I found myself signing up for Pre-calculus and Advanced Quadratic Equations.

Back then, before Canva, AI, and all these instant-access design tools, Photoshop was *IT*. And even that felt like a far-off dream—an untouchable world I wasn't sure I could break into.

So, I buried that creative spark, telling myself I needed to be "practical." I tried to silence the part of me that lit up whenever I sketched, painted, or imagined something new.

But here's the thing: when you're built for something, you can't keep it buried.

Fast forward to college, and I finally let myself dive into design fully. That's when everything changed. My professors noticed. My classmates noticed. My work wasn't just good—it was exceptional. From drawings to paintings to design projects, everything I created stood out. My work consistently topped the class, and I realized I'd found my gift.

By sophomore year, I wasn't just keeping up—I was leading the way. Out of thousands of designers nationwide, I won first place in a major competition for Chrysler and John Varvatos. At nineteen, I was walking the red carpet in LA, rubbing shoulders with Jennifer Garner and Ben Affleck, with a $6,000 check in my pocket and a suite in a four-star hotel.

The icing on the cake? Meeting the Chrysler design team behind the 200c John Varvatos limited edition—the same kind of creatives I once thought I'd never measure up to.

That's when it hit me: My "problem" was never loving art too much. My weakness wasn't being too creative. The only real weakness was thinking I needed to dim my light to fit in.

And that's the truth about strength—sometimes, your greatest power is the very thing you're told to tone down. Those instincts you're asked to suppress? That passion you're told to scale back? That's your superpower waiting to be unleashed.

3. Passions: Your Natural Energy

Let me show you what real passion looks like. 10:30 PM on a Saturday night. I'm in my room, locked in—not because I have to be, but because I *can't not be*. On one screen I have After Effects tutorials, another screen scrolls through the latest design trends. A third dives deep into Photoshop while 432Hz frequencies hum softly in the background, keeping me steady. My phone buzzes relentlessly, notifications piling up. But I haven't blinked, let alone had time to check it.

Friends ask where I've gone, why I don't go out anymore, why I've 'changed.' They don't understand, and maybe they never will. Passion doesn't ask for permission—it takes over, pulls you in, and doesn't let go. When you find your real passion, it's not a choice. It's a possession. Most people talk about passion like it's this gentle, comfortable thing. Like finding a nice hobby or something that "brings you joy."

Bullshit.

Real passion is inconvenient. It's disruptive. It makes you look crazy to normal people. It has you missing parties, skipping hangouts, missing birthdays, diving into depths that seem excessive to everyone else.

I'd come home from my day job and immediately jump back on my computer. Not because I had to – because my future depended on it.

Even after my first real heartbreak - losing my college sweetheart - I didn't spiral. I immediately got to work and designed and launched my entire first season of NO DOUBT APPAREL™. Because even when my heart was broken, my passion still burned. That flame inside? It never goes out.

That's the difference between interest and passion:

- Interest watches the clock, counting minutes until it can stop
- Passion loses track of time, shocked when the sun comes up

Interest asks "What's the minimum I need to learn?"
Passion asks "How deep down this rabbit hole can I go?"
Interest says "That's good enough."
Passion says "What if we pushed it further?"

Here's your wake-up call: If you're forcing yourself to be passionate about something, it might not be your passion at all—it could be a vision handed to you by society, others' expectations, or even an unexamined part of yourself. When you find your real passion, you don't need motivation. You need someone to tell you to go to sleep. You don't need deadlines. You need boundaries. You don't need push notifications. You need someone to remind you to eat.

Look at your life right now. What keeps you up at night? What makes you forget to eat? What makes you lose track of time? That's not your problem to fix - that's your passion trying to tell you something.

4. Purpose: The Fire Inside

There's this moment, right after hitting rock bottom, when the world gets real quiet. When all the noise of "should" and "supposed to" fades away, and you're left with nothing but truth.

My moment came during the twilight hours in my mom's basement. Not rock star rock bottom. Not dramatic movie rock bottom. Just... sitting there, $0 to my name, surrounded by half-eaten ramen packages and a mountain of self-doubt. My computer screens are still glowing from another all-night design session and a halfway completed business plan.

That's when it hit me. This wasn't just about making logos anymore. This wasn't just about design. This was about all those people feeling what I felt. All those souls dimming their light because the world told them they were "too much." All those dreams dying quietly because someone said "be realistic."

Purpose isn't some mystical destiny that falls from the sky. It's not a career path or a five-year plan or whatever bullshit Instagram quotes tell you it is.

Purpose is what happens when your values, strengths, and passions align with something bigger than yourself. When that energy that people called "too much" finally finds its reason. When those late nights of creation finally find their cause.

For me, it clicked when I started seeing how my designs affected people. Not just aesthetically, but emotionally. My work wasn't just about looking good anymore - it was about making people feel something. Making them believe something. About themselves. About their possibilities. About their power.

Purpose is what makes you clench your fists at 6 AM and say "This isn't how our story ends."

It's what makes you look at mediocrity and say "We deserve more than this."

It's what makes you stare into the darkness of self-doubt and say "Watch us rise."

Because here's what nobody tells you about purpose: It's not about what you want to do. It's not even about what you're good at. It's about the impact only you can make. The lives only you can touch. The change only you can create.

I spent years thinking purpose had to be something grand. Something world-changing. But real purpose? It starts with one person. One idea. One message that says "I see you. I feel you. And we're not settling for less anymore."

Key Takeaways:

- True self-knowledge comes from confronting your deepest truths and fears
- Your values aren't what you claim - they're what you live
- Real passion isn't comfortable - it's all consuming
- Purpose emerges when values, strengths, and passions align

Your Turn:

1. Complete the Values Audit (what decisions reflect your real values?)

2. Track your energy for one week (what makes you lose track of time?)

3. Write your truth statement (who are you when no one's watching?)

What's Next: Our journey continues as we explore how external validation can mask our true identity.

2

Best Dressed & Depressed: The Illusion of Success

"To be yourself in a world that is constantly trying to make you something else is the greatest accomplishment."
— Ralph Waldo Emerson

5:30 AM. Another morning spent orchestrating the perfect shield. Let me be clear - this wasn't about vanity. When you're the short nerdy kid with glasses who gets good grades, you learn to minimize targets. I couldn't change my height. Couldn't ditch the glasses. Wasn't about to tank my GPA. But my wardrobe? That I could control.

And here's the thing - what started as armor became artistry. I might have been the short 'smart kid', but no one could touch my style game. Not designer labels or expensive brands. Just pure, authentic creativity. Calculated combinations that made even the haters pause.

It may have started as my weakness, but I turned it into my super-power. Every perfectly coordinated fit was a silent comeback to every joke, every jab, every sideways comment. They could laugh at my grades or my glasses, but they couldn't deny my eye for style.

But that's the thing about armor - it gets heavy.

By the time senior year rolled around, I had mastered the art of looking untouchable. Best Dressed in the yearbook? Check. On the surface, I was the epitome of confidence. But inside? I was drained. Not just from the 5:30 AM wardrobe sessions, but from the soul-crushing weight of keeping up the performance.

The cruel irony was that I couldn't stand the person staring back at me in the mirror. No matter how much I tried to fit in, my own doubt held me back. I didn't believe I was 'cool' enough—not really. That doubt became a wall, keeping me from joining groups, quitting sports I once loved, and walking away from opportunities that could've been mine. It wasn't just a lack of belief—it was a self-imposed exile.

The Breaking Point

You want to know what real exhaustion feels like? It's not just physical, it's spiritual too. It's standing in front of your mirror at 3 AM after another night of surface-level conversations and hollow laughter, realizing you've gotten so good at playing a role that you've forgotten who you actually are.

I had become what I thought others wanted me to be:

- The guy who always looked put together
- The one who never wanted to be caught off guard

• The master of keeping up appearances

But at what cost?

The Hampton Revolution

Then came Hampton University. And something magical happened—I stepped onto that campus and realized: nobody here knew me. Nobody had any expectations. Nobody was waiting to take shots. For the first time in my life, I could just... be.

So I did something radical: I stopped trying so hard.

I didn't stop caring completely—I still believed in making a strong first impression and keeping myself put together. But I stopped obsessing over what others thought. Instead of perfect outfits as armor, I let my style become an authentic extension of me.

I started wearing what felt good, not just what looked "perfect." I let my nerdy flag fly without apology. And you know what happened? People responded to the authenticity—not because I was trying to impress them, but because I wasn't.

Remember that "Best Dressed" title from high school? At Hampton, I ended up becoming known for something much more valuable - being real. Being someone who encouraged others to embrace their quirks, chase their passions, and stop apologizing for taking up space.

The Transformation Blueprint

Let me show you exactly how this transformation happens, because trust me - if I could break free from years of performing, so can you.

Recognize Your Armor
- What are you using as a shield?
- What parts of yourself are you hiding?
- What masks have become so comfortable you've forgotten they're masks?

Find Your Fresh Start
- You don't need a new school or city
- Start with one small area of your life
- Give yourself permission to experiment

Cut the Act
- Stop calculating every move
- Let your natural interests show
- Allow yourself to be imperfect

Build Authentic Connections
- Connect through real interests
- Share your genuine passions
- Let your enthusiasm attract your tribe

The Real Power

Here's what nobody tells you about authenticity - it's not just about "being yourself." It's about freeing up all the energy you've been using to be someone else.

Think about it:

- The mental space taken up by constant calculation
- The emotional energy drained by perpetual performance
- The life force wasted on maintaining facades

What could you do with all that energy if you redirected it toward actual growth instead of keeping up appearances?

Your Turn: The Freedom Challenge

Start here:

1. Pick one area of your life where you're "performing."
2. Give yourself permission to drop the act for one day
3. Notice how much energy you reclaim
4. Reinvest that energy in something real

Remember: Breaking free from the act isn't about not caring - it's about caring about the right things. It's about redirecting your energy from keeping up appearances to building something real.

You don't have to do it all at once. Start small. Start today. Start with one moment of choosing authenticity over approval.

Because here's the truth: The world doesn't need your perfection. It needs your authenticity. It needs your real voice, your real passions, your real power.

Let's get it.

Key Takeaways:

- Armor that once protected you can become your prison
- Authenticity isn't about not caring - it's about caring about what matters
- External validation is temporary - internal alignment is permanent
- Real style comes from expressing yourself, not impressing others

Your Turn: The Freedom Challenge

1. Pick one area of your life where you're "performing"
2. Give yourself permission to drop the act for one day
3. Notice how much energy you reclaim
4. Reinvest that energy in something real

What's Next: Discover how emotional intelligence emerges from our deepest wounds.

3

From Pain to Power - A Lesson in EQ

The phone rings.

My heart skips a beat. Something feels... off. You know that moment when your body knows before your mind catches up? When your cells are screaming that everything's about to change?

I answered, "Hello?"

My mom's voice trembles: "No one has seen or heard from your brother in over two weeks."

The date was November 23rd. My birthday. But birthdays don't matter when your world is shattering into a million razor-sharp pieces.

The Breaking

Have you ever watched your life split in two? Not metaphorically. Physically.

I watched my knees hit the floor in slow motion, felt the carpet dig into my palms, heard the sound trying to claw its way out of my throat but getting stuck somewhere between my heart and my lips.

The human body isn't designed to handle certain kinds of pain. Not the kind that rewires your DNA. Not the kind that splits your existence into a "before" and "after." Not the kind that makes you question every moment you thought you had more time for.

What followed that phone call wasn't just a search for my brother. It was an unwanted masterclass in human emotion - the kind they don't teach you about in school:

The *hope* that burns your throat at 3 AM while you're calling another hospital, bargaining with God, with the universe, with anyone who might be listening. *"Please, just let him be okay. I'll do anything."*

The *anger* that makes your fingers shake while typing another social media post. "Has anyone seen my brother Daniel Redd?" Delete. Type. Delete. How do you compress a lifetime of love into a Facebook status?

The *guilt* that crushes your chest when you try to sleep, every memory playing on repeat. Should I have called more? Visited more? Known somehow?

Then the devastating silence when your phone finally rings with news, but not the news you prayed for.

The Awakening

They found his body in the river. Right there in our hometown. The same waters we'd passed by countless times, laughing, living, never knowing they would become sacred ground.

In those first few days, time became meaningless. The world blurred into a series of disconnected moments:

- Family members arriving
- Phones ringing
- Voices trying to comfort
- Questions needing answers

And that's when something inside me... shifted.

Through the fog of those first days, two questions kept echoing in my mind: "Who is hurting inside?" "Where is the hurt?"

Not philosophical questions. Survival questions.

Because the pain lived everywhere - I wanted to scream, but no sound came out. I wanted to run, but my legs wouldn't move. The world kept spinning as if nothing had changed, but everything had changed. Everything.

The pain was sharp, deep, hot, jagged, raw, and swift - and it showed no mercy. It pierced my heart with an intensity that took my breath away. I was weak and severely wounded. My reality had been invaded by darkness, and it had successfully claimed a life, right from under my nose. And in trying to locate it, to map its jagged edges, I stumbled upon something powerful:

Pain has geography.

Every emotion lives somewhere specific in your body. And when you can map it, you can move it.

The Discovery

Three months after losing him I'm curled up on my bedroom floor, grief hitting in waves. But this time was different. Instead of fighting the tsunami, I started studying it.

"Where exactly are you?"
"What are you trying to tell me?"
"What do you need right now?"

That's when I discovered what I now call the *2-Minute Emotional Release Technique*.

Here's exactly how it works:

When intense emotions hit - whether it's grief, anger, fear, whatever - set a timer for 2-3 minutes.

During this time, feel everything. Let it all out. Scream into a pillow. Bite down on this book if you have to (just buy another copy after). Do whatever you need to express that emotion fully (in a safe way).

But here's the crucial part - when that timer goes off, you're done. Let it go.

Why? Because emotions are like pressure in a valve. Keep them pent up, they'll destroy you from inside. Let them flow uncontrolled, they'll drown you. But release them with intention, with purpose? That's where the power lives.

First minute: *Pure, raw pain*
Second minute: *The pain starts to move*
Third minute: *Something shifts*

When that timer goes off, the pain isn't gone - but it's transformed from a tsunami into a wave you can ride.

The Alchemy

Here's what nobody tells you about deep loss - it doesn't just break you open. It breaks you open to depths you never knew you had.

Think about this: If you can feel this much pain... How much joy might you be capable of? If you can survive this much darkness... How much light might you be able to hold?

The Power Shift

4 AM. The world sleeps while I'm deep in meditation on my bedroom floor. Not because I'm some guru or yogi, but because pain this deep demands to be understood, it demands my attention.

Here's what I discovered in those dark hours that changed everything:

The Emotional Map

Grief lives in your chest - a black hole trying to collapse your ribs. Anger burns in your jaw - electricity looking for ground. Fear freezes in your gut - ice spreading through your veins. Guilt crushes your shoulders - weight that makes Atlas look lazy.

But here's the thing about mapping pain - once you know its geography, you can start redrawing the borders.

The System

Let me show you exactly how to turn your deepest pain into rocket fuel:

1. Locate the Feeling

When emotion hits:

- Plant your feet on the ground
- Place one hand where it hurts most
- Close your eyes
- Name it. Out loud.

"Hello, grief. I see you trying to collapse my chest." "Hey, anger. I feel you burning in my hands." "There you are, fear. Ice in my stomach again."

Sound crazy? Good. Sanity never changed anyone's life.

2. The Release Valve

Set your timer:

- First minute: Feel everything
- Second minute: Let it move
- Third minute: Watch it transform

Don't just read this. Do it. Right now.
Feel that knot in your throat? That pressure in your chest? Set your timer. I'll wait.

3. The Alchemist's Secret

Here's what they don't tell you about emotional intelligence - it's not about being calm. It's about being powerful.

Every emotion becomes:

- A data point to read rooms
- A radar to sense lies
- A compass for truth
- A weapon for change

After losing my brother, I could walk into any meeting and instantly read:

- The tension no one mentions

- The fear behind the bravado
- The truth behind the masks
- The pain behind the power

Not because I'm special. Because pain has taught me to see what others spend their lives avoiding. I was allowing myself to feel all the emotion and energy in a room without it overwhelming me.

The 21-Day Emotional Mapping Practice

This is your systematic approach to mastering emotional intelligence. For the next 21 days:

Morning Scan (5 minutes):

- Where does your anxiety live?
- What's that excitement in your chest?
- Name it. Face it. Use it.

Trigger Moments:

- Set your timer
- Feel fully
- Write it down
- Track the patterns

Power Integration:

- Turn grief into gratitude

- Transform anger into action
- Use fear as fuel
- Make pain your power

The Real Power

Want to know what real emotional intelligence looks like in action? It's not just being aware of feelings—it's being attuned to the undercurrents no one talks about but everyone feels. It's walking into a room and knowing:

Who's on the verge of walking away, even before they've admitted it to themselves.

Which relationship is hanging by a thread, fraying in ways they can't quite name.

What deal is doomed to collapse because the trust it's built on is already cracking.

Who's silently screaming for help, even as they wear a brave face.

It's not magic, and it's not psychic. It's the result of learning to sit with discomfort—theirs and your own—and read the emotional truths most people spend their lives avoiding. It's seeing what's unsaid, what's hidden beneath polite smiles and nods. Because once you stop running from your own emotions, you begin to recognize everyone else's.

The Advanced Protocol

Here's how to navigate the highest-stakes moments with mastery:

1. The Deep Read (Before the moment)
- Arrive early—feel the energy of the empty space before it fills.
- Watch people enter and observe their "emotional weather"—their moods, hesitations, and intentions.
- Track the subtle shifts as the atmosphere begins to change.

This is your foundation: the unseen dynamics beneath the surface.

2. The Power Move (When tension peaks)
- Anchor yourself in your truth first—calm, clear, unshakable.
- Identify the pain points others are avoiding.
- Name the elephant in the room—not to create discomfort, but to release it.
- Hold space for the storm—let emotions rise without letting them control the room.
- Then, guide the transformation: shift the focus, propose solutions, or offer clarity.

This is where you turn chaos into connection.

3. The Integration (After the moment)
- Reflect: What did you feel? What patterns emerged?
- Analyze: What actions shifted the dynamic? What stayed stuck?
- Document: Add this moment to your "emotional database"—your growing intuition for handling what comes next.

Mastery comes in the follow-through: learning from every moment to sharpen your instincts for the next.

Mapping Your Emotional Geography

Emotions are not just abstract feelings; they are deeply intertwined with physical sensations in the body. While emotions are processed in the brain—specifically in areas like the amygdala, insula, and prefrontal cortex—they often manifest physically through the autonomic nervous system. Understanding where and how emotions show up in your body can be a powerful tool for emotional awareness and self-regulation.

Research has shown that emotions activate specific regions in the body. A 2014 study published in the *Proceedings of the National Academy of Sciences* used "body maps" to identify where participants commonly felt emotions. The findings revealed consistent activation patterns for different emotions across individuals. The vagus nerve, which connects the brain to various organs, plays a significant role in how emotions are expressed physically, particularly in the chest and stomach.

Here's a guide to how emotions are commonly experienced in the body:

1. **Fear**
   - **Location:** Chest, stomach
   - **Sensation:** Tightness, rapid heartbeat, butterflies in the stomach
   - **Reason:** Activation of the fight-or-flight response, preparing the body for action.

2. **Anger**
   - **Location:** Chest, head, arms
   - **Sensation:** Heat or pressure in the chest, tension in the jaw, neck, or fists

- **Reason:** Increased blood flow and muscle tension, preparing for confrontation.

3. **Sadness**
    - **Location:** Chest, eyes, throat
    - **Sensation:** Heaviness in the chest, lump in the throat, teary eyes
    - **Reason:** The body's response to emotional pain or loss.

4. **Happiness**
    - **Location:** Chest, face
    - **Sensation:** Lightness, warmth in the chest, smiling muscles activated
    - **Reason:** Release of dopamine and endorphins, creating positive sensations.

5. **Anxiety**
    - **Location:** Stomach, chest
    - **Sensation:** Nausea, tightness, restlessness
    - **Reason:** Activation of the stress response, affecting digestion and breathing.

6. **Love**
    - **Location:** Chest, stomach
    - **Sensation:** Warmth, fluttering sensation in the stomach (often called butterflies)
    - **Reason:** Hormones like oxytocin create positive physical sensations.

7. **Shame or Embarrassment**
    - **Location:** Face, neck

- **Sensation:** Blushing, warmth, or heat in the face and neck
- **Reason:** Increased blood flow to the face due to a perceived social threat.

8. **Gratitude**
   - **Location:** Chest, shoulders
   - **Sensation:** Warmth, openness, relaxation
   - **Reason:** Positive emotions counteract stress and promote calmness.

Recognizing these patterns can help you better understand your emotional state and manage your reactions. Techniques such as deep breathing, mindfulness, and progressive muscle relaxation can be used to regulate these physical sensations, offering relief and clarity in moments of intense emotion.

The Ultimate Truth

Another 3 AM. Another sleepless night after losing my brother. But this time, something different happens. I realize: Pain this deep doesn't just break you open. It breaks you open to depths you never knew you had. If you can survive this much hurt... If you can navigate these dark waters... If you can transform this much pain into power...What else might you be capable of?

Because here's the truth that changed everything: Your greatest pain isn't your weakness. It's your PhD in human nature. Your master's degree in what really matters. Your doctorate in depth most people spend their lives avoiding. Every tear becomes a teaching. Every breakdown becomes a breakthrough. Every wound becomes wisdom.

This isn't just about surviving pain anymore. It's about turning that pain into a superpower that changes every room you enter, every life you touch, every move you make. Your pain isn't your enemy. It's your edge. Your secret weapon. Your gift to a world that desperately needs people who aren't afraid to feel everything.

Now get out there and show them what real power looks like.

Let's get it.

Key Takeaways:

- Pain isn't just something to endure - it's something to transform
- Every emotion has a physical location in your body
- Emotional intelligence isn't about being calm - it's about being powerful
- Your greatest pain can become your greatest power

Your Turn:

1. Map your emotional geography (where do you feel different emotions?)
2. Practice the 2-Minute Release Technique daily
3. Start building your emotional database
4. Use one pain point as fuel for transformation

What's Next: We'll explore how breaking through limitations requires more than just motivation - it demands systematic deconstruction of our mental barriers.

PART II: BREAKING THROUGH

Awakening is just the beginning. Breaking through is where the real work begins—the hard, gritty battle to demolish the walls holding you back. It's the process of facing your limitations, silencing the doubt, and committing to the systems and habits that will carry you forward.

In these next four chapters, you'll see how I challenged my own beliefs, rewired my thinking, and adopted practices that transformed frustration into focus. You'll witness how breaking down old patterns created the space for something entirely new to emerge.

But this isn't just about my journey; it's about yours. As you read, think about the barriers you've accepted as unmovable and the opportunities you've left unexplored. What would it mean to push just a little harder, to refuse to settle, to keep moving even when it gets uncomfortable?

Breaking through isn't easy, but it's where the magic happens. Because on the other side of resistance is power—your power, waiting to be unlocked.

Let's get to work.

4

Cracking the Code: Unlocking Your Mind

Picture this: I'm lounging in my parents' living room, eyes scanning the clutter of familiar objects, when something catches my attention. My little sister's Rubik's Cube. Just another piece of plastic collecting dust. Another impossible puzzle that "smart people" solve.

But something feels different tonight. Maybe it's the echo of another day designing car advertisements. Maybe it's the weight of dreams deferred. Maybe it's just time.

"You've got to be Einstein to solve those, right?"

The thought appears automatically, and in that moment, I catch myself. I caught the lie. I caught the limitation forming before it could take root.

Without thinking, I grab the cube and make a quiet vow to myself: "I won't stop until I learn how to figure this out."

The Challenge Begins

First stop: YouTube: "How to solve Rubik's Cube for beginners"

You want to talk about humbling? Try watching a 9-year-old solve it blindfolded, with his feet, while jumping on a trampoline. There I am, a grown man, fumbling with this cube like a monkey trying to solve quantum physics, while some kids' basically doing calculus with his toes.

But did that stop me? Hell no. If anything, it made me more determined. I figured if a fourth-grader could do it with his toes while blindfolded, surely I, a fully grown adult with opposable thumbs and functioning eyesight, could manage it, eventually.

Every day after work I would practice for at least 30 minutes. Thirty minutes becomes two hours. Two hours become three. The cube became my obsession, my nemesis, my teacher. I'd make progress, get stuck on the last piece, make one wrong move, and watch everything scramble back to chaos.

By week two, I was bringing it to work. It would sit on my desk between car advertisements and grocery store flyers, a constant reminder of either my determination or my insanity - I'm not sure which anymore.

Eventually my co-workers even started to take notice:

"What's that you got there? Is that a Rubik's cube?"
"Can you solve that?"
"Don't you have to be a genius?"

"I know a kid who can solve it blindfolded with his toes..."

Then comes the moment. Lunch break. The fluorescent lights humming overhead like a countdown timer, and one of my coworkers watches me working through another attempt. The question that changes everything:

"Nick, are you EVER gonna solve that thing?"

Was that a challenge? Big mistake. The new me incubating inside is chomping at the bit to yell, "I'LL SHOW YOU!!!!" But I calmly and simply replied, "Yup. And I'll solve it for you RIGHT. NOW."

Up to this point, I'd never been able to figure out the last move. But in that moment, something shifts. The doubt evaporates. The fear burns away. A fire ignites in my chest that I'd never felt before.

Three sets of eyes watching my every move. Every twist, every turn, carrying the weight of transformation. It feels like a shot clock buzzer-beater going off in my head.

"3" *twist* "2!" *twist* "annndd..... 1" *Twist to completion*

"HELLL YEAH!"

The table erupted with joy! I had just solved my first Rubik's cube! The child-like toy that had stumped generations for decades was now mine to claim. I was overjoyed. To know that I didn't give up, that I kept going, and that I had successfully broken a self-limiting belief, live in person!

But it didn't stop there. Once I solved it once, I solved it twice, 5 times, 10, 50 times. I even started an Excel sheet with one of my co-workers to track my speed every Friday to see how fast I could do it! (My best time was 2 minutes and 8 seconds.)

THE REAL BREAKTHROUGH

But here's what happens when you crack through one limiting belief - you get hungry for more. That solved cube sitting on my desk wasn't just a completed puzzle anymore. It became evidence. Proof that the stories I'd been telling myself were just that - stories.

Let me show you exactly how this transformation happened:

Phase 1: The Commitment

Day 1-3: Pure frustration and jumbled moves
Day 4-7: Learning basic patterns
Day 8-14: Building muscle memory
Day 15+: Starting to see the cube differently

Every day after work, I'd sit down for 30-45 mins with:

- YouTube tutorials playing
- Notes scattered around
- Timer on my phone
- Pure determination in my gut

Phase 2: The System

I broke it down into manageable pieces:

1. Master the first layer
2. Learn middle layer patterns
3. Tackle final layer algorithms
4. Track every attempt

Here's what nobody tells you about mastering anything - it's not about the end goal. It's about falling in love with the process.

The Excel Sheet Revolution

That Excel sheet my coworker and I created? It became more than just numbers. Each entry told a story:

Week 1: 15 minutes average
Week 4: 8 minutes
Week 8: 4.5 minutes

Final Best: 2 minutes, 8 seconds

But the real victory wasn't in the times - it was in the transformation happening inside my mind. With each improvement, another limiting belief shattered:

"I'm not good at patterns" - **SHATTERED**
"I don't have time" - **BUSTED**
"I can't learn complex systems" - **BROKEN**
"I'm not smart enough for this" - **DESTROYED**

The NO DOUBT Method for Breaking Limitations

Here's exactly how to crack your own code:

1. **Identify Your Cube**

   - What's your "impossible" challenge?
   - What's the limiting belief holding you back?
   - What's the story you've been telling yourself?

1. **Break It Down**

   - What's the smallest first step?
   - What's one pattern you can master?
   - What's one small win you can achieve?

1. **Create Your System**

   - Daily practice time
   - Progress tracking method
   - Accountability structure

1. **Push Through Plateaus**

   - Expect resistance
   - Plan for setbacks
   - Keep showing up

The Bigger Picture

This isn't just about solving puzzles. It's about:

- Breaking mental barriers
- Building confidence through evidence
- Creating momentum for bigger challenges

Think about it - what's your Rubik's Cube right now? What challenge have you decided is "for other people" but not for you?

- Maybe it's starting that business
- Maybe it's learning that skill
- Maybe it's making that change

Your NO DOUBT Challenge

Here's your blueprint for breaking free:

1. **This Week:**

- Buy your own Rubik's Cube (Like today!)
- Set aside daily practice time
- Create a tracking system

1. **First 30 Days:**

- Document every attempt
- Celebrate small victories
- Build evidence of capability

1. **Beyond:**

- Use this success as fuel
- Target bigger limitations
- Keep breaking barriers

The Ultimate Truth

Remember this: That Rubik's Cube still sits on my desk (I have about 4 of them now). Not as a trophy, but as a reminder. A reminder that every limitation is just a story waiting to be rewritten. Every "impossible" is just a challenge waiting to be cracked.

Because once you break through one limitation, you realize something powerful: The only real prison is the one you build in your mind. And you hold the key to every door.

Let's get it.

Key Takeaways:

- Limiting beliefs are just stories we tell ourselves
- Breaking one limitation creates momentum for breaking others
- Success leaves evidence - track your progress
- Systems beat motivation every time

Your Turn:

1. Identify your current "Rubik's Cube" (what seems impossible?)

2. Break it down into learnable patterns
3. Create your tracking system
4. Commit to daily practice

What's Next: We'll explore how deep work becomes your ultimate weapon in achieving what others call impossible.

5

The Deep Work Manifesto

Picture two very different days in my life...

Day One: I'm at my corporate job, designing ads for a local media company. My phone buzzes every few minutes. Email notifications pop up constantly. Coworkers stop by to chat. I'm "working" for eight hours, but by the end of the day, I've only managed to create two basic ad designs. I feel drained, unfulfilled, and somehow still behind.

Day Two: It's 4:30 AM in my mom's basement. My phone is in airplane mode. The world is quiet. For the next three hours, I'm studying crypto patterns, analyzing market trends, and making strategic trades. In this focused state, I make more progress in three hours than I used to make in a week.

The difference? Deep work.

Breaking Free from Butterfly Mode

Most people never tap into their true potential because they live in what I call "butterfly mode" – fluttering from task to task, never fully landing anywhere. They're:

- Checking emails while on calls
- Scrolling social media during meetings
- Responding to every notification
- Living at the mercy of their devices

I know, because I was one of them.

But here's the truth: Your ability to focus deeply isn't just another skill. It's a superpower. And in today's distracted world, it's becoming increasingly rare and increasingly valuable.

The Wake-Up Call

My journey to deep work began out of necessity. After quitting my job at Forever 21 after returning from Korea, I knew I needed a change. But it wasn't just about working harder – I'd tried that before. It was about working deeper.

So I established a daily routine:

- 4:30 AM wake-up
- Phone in airplane mode
- No distractions, no exceptions
- Focused blocks of uninterrupted learning and work

At first, it was torture. My mind, addicted to constant stimulation, rebelled. I'd reach for my phone without thinking. I'd find any excuse to break focus. But I persisted, because I had to. This wasn't just about productivity – it was about transformation.

The Digital Detox Reality Check

Let me tell you about my first week of digital detox. It was during my 21-day commitment period after leaving Forever 21. I decided to track how many times I mindlessly reached for my phone.

Day one: *113 times.*

I was shocked. But what was even more shocking? Most of those reaches weren't even for anything important. They were just habits – a nervous tick, an addiction to distraction.

Here's what I learned: Your phone isn't just a device; it's a dopamine delivery system. Every notification, every scroll, every like gives you a tiny hit of that feel-good chemical. And like any addiction, it's destroying your ability to focus.

The Focus First Protocol

The solution wasn't going cold turkey. Instead, I developed what I call the Focus First Protocol:

Morning Sanctuary
- No phone for the first 3 hours of the day
- This is your time to set intentions
- Deep work and momentum building only

Airplane Mode Blocks
- Schedule 90-minute deep work sessions
- Phone in airplane mode, no exceptions
- Complete isolation from digital distractions

Notification Audit
- Delete all non-essential apps
- Turn off all notifications except calls from key people
- Create barriers between you and distraction

Digital Sunset
- No screens 1 hour before bed
- Your brain needs time to wind down
- Prepare for the next day's deep work

Building Your Focus Muscle

During my trading days, I discovered something crucial: Focus isn't just about eliminating distractions. It's about training your mind to stay engaged with complex problems for extended periods.

Think of it like building physical strength – you don't start by trying to lift 300 pounds. You start with what you can handle and progressively increase the load.

Here's how I built my focus muscle:

Level 1: The 25-Minute Sprint
- Start with 25 minutes of focused work
- Take a 5-minute break
- Repeat 4 times
- Track how many times your mind wanders

I remember my first 25-minute session studying crypto patterns. My mind bounced around like a pinball. But I kept at it, marking down every time I got distracted. Each session, those marks became fewer.

Level 2: The 45-Minute Deep Dive
- Extend focus periods to 45 minutes
- Take 10-minute breaks
- Add complexity to your tasks
- Journal your insights during breaks

This is where I started seeing real gains. By this point, I could analyze market trends without my mind drifting to Instagram or what I was having for lunch.

Level 3: The 90-Minute Flow State
- Full 90-minute deep work sessions
- Design environment for zero distractions
- Tackle your most challenging work
- Document breakthrough moments

At this level, something magical happens. Time disappears. Work becomes effortless. Solutions come naturally. This is where I made my biggest crypto gains – not because I was smarter than everyone else, but because I could focus longer and deeper than most.

Creating Your Deep Work Sanctuary

Let me paint you a picture of my mom's basement setup. Not glamorous, but it was my laboratory for focus:

- Desk facing a blank wall
- Single lamp for focused lighting
- Phone charging in another room
- Water bottle and notepad within arm's reach
- Noise-canceling headphones ready

This wasn't just a workspace – it was a focus factory. Every element was designed with one purpose: to enable deep work.

The Four Levels of Work

Through my journey, I've identified four distinct levels of work. Understanding these changed how I approach every task:

Level 1: Shallow Work
- Email checking
- Basic admin tasks
- Social media

- Low-value, reactive activities

This is where most people spend their entire day. It feels busy, but produces little real value.

Level 2: Semi-Focused Work
- Basic content creation
- Routine problem solving
- Regular business operations
- Requires some concentration

I used to think this was "deep work." I was wrong.

Level 3: Deep Work
- Strategic planning
- Complex problem solving
- Creative breakthroughs
- High-value, focused activities

This is where the magic starts happening. This is where I cracked the crypto patterns that led to real gains.

Level 4: Flow State
- Complete immersion
- Time disappears
- Peak performance
- Breakthrough insights

This is the holy grail. When you hit this state, three hours feel like minutes, and you can accomplish what usually takes days.

Your goal? Maximize time in Levels 3 and 4. Everything else can be delegated, automated, or eliminated.

The NO DOUBT Deep Work System

Here's my proven system, refined through countless early morning sessions:

Morning Power Block (4:30 AM - 7:30 AM)

First 30 minutes:

- Meditation and intention setting
- No phone, no distractions
- Clear mind, clear purpose

Next 2.5 hours:

- Most important task of the day
- Complete isolation from the world
- Pure, uninterrupted focus

This is when I'd study market patterns, identify opportunities, and make my biggest trades. Why? Because while others were sleeping, I was putting in focused work that would compound throughout the day.

Strategic Breaks (7:30 AM - 8:00 AM)
- Physical movement (push-ups or going for a run or walk are great)

- Hydration and nutrition
- Quick journal entry of insights
- Mental reset for next session

Think of these breaks like intervals in a workout. They're not about checking Instagram – they're about optimizing your mind for the next round of deep work.

Second Deep Session (8:00 AM - 9:30 AM)
- Different but related task
- Build on morning momentum
- Document patterns and insights
- Keep the flow going

During my crypto days, this is when I'd go over what I'd learned in the morning session. Theory became practice. Ideas became action.

Integration Period (9:30 AM - 10:00 AM)
- Review progress
- Plan next deep work session
- Limited communication check
- Set up for success

By this time, I'd accomplished more than most people do in a full day. Not because I'm special – because I protected my deep work time like my life depended on it

Breaking Through Common Obstacles

Let me share the real obstacles I faced and how I overcame them:

"I'm Not a Morning Person"

I wasn't either. When I first started waking up at 4:30 AM, it felt like torture. Here's what worked:

- No gradual transition. Set your alarm for 4:30 AM and commit. (Helpful Tip: Use the **5 Second Rule** by Mel Robbins. When your alarm goes off, don't think about it. Just countdown 5-4-3-2-1 and get up – physically move and stand on your feet. This simple trick interrupts hesitation and propels you into action.)
- Put your alarm across the room.
- Have your clothes laid out the night before.
- Remember: The pain is temporary, the gains are permanent.

"I Can't Focus That Long"

Truth: Nobody can at first. Your focus muscle is like any other – it needs training.
Start here:

- 25 minutes of pure focus
- Track your distractions
- Celebrate small wins
- Build gradually

I went from barely managing 25 minutes to flowing for 3 hours straight. It's possible.

"There Are Too Many Interruptions"

This was my biggest challenge during crypto trading. The solution?

- Communicate your deep work times to everyone
- Create physical barriers (closed door, headphones)
- Set clear boundaries ("I'm unavailable until 9:30 AM")
- Batch shallow tasks for later

"I Don't Have Time"

Here's the brutal truth: You do have time. You're just spending it on shallow work and distractions.

When I tracked my time:

- 2 hours on social media
- 1 hour reacting to emails
- 45 minutes on pointless meetings
- Countless moments of useless scrolling

That's 4+ hours I could redirect to deep work.

The secret isn't finding more time – it's protecting the time you have.

Making Deep Work Your Lifestyle

This isn't about a temporary productivity hack. It's about fundamentally changing how you operate in the world. Here's what that looks like:

The Deep Work Lifestyle

Morning Ritual:

- Wake up at 4:30 AM
- No phone until after deep work
- Pure focus, no compromises
- Build momentum early

Environment Design:

- Dedicated workspace
- Minimal distractions
- Tools ready
- Clear entry/exit cues

Digital Boundaries:

- Airplane mode during deep work
- No social media before noon
- Email batching twice daily
- Strategic technology use

The Compound Effect

Let me show you what this compound effect looks like:

One Deep Work Session:

- 3 hours of focused work
- Clear mind, clear purpose

- Breakthrough insights
- Momentum building

One Week of Deep Work:

- 15 hours of pure focus
- Major progress on key projects
- Increased mental clarity
- Growing confidence

One Month of Deep Work:

- 60 hours of breakthrough work
- Visible results
- New opportunities
- Transformed capabilities

This is how I went from counting bodies at Forever 21 to building a six-figure business. Not through talent or luck, but through consistent, focused deep work.

The Ultimate Truth

Deep work isn't just about productivity. It's about respect for your time, your potential, and your dreams.

Every time you choose focus over distraction, you're saying:

- My goals matter
- My dreams matter
- My time matters

- My potential matters

Remember: While others are scrolling, you're growing. While they're reacting, you're creating. While they're distracted, you're directed.
This is your edge. Your superpower. Your path to breaking through. Let's get it.

Key Takeaways:

- Deep work isn't a skill - it's a superpower
- Focus is a muscle that must be trained systematically
- Environment shapes behavior - design for success
- The compound effect of deep work transforms everything

Your Turn:

1. Design your deep work sanctuary
2. Implement the Focus First Protocol
3. Track your focus progress daily
4. Choose one deep work block to protect

What's Next: We'll discover how the right money mindset transforms every-thing about your success.

6

Money Mindset (A Crypto Story)

Have you ever had one of those moments where you realize something has to change—not just a little, but everything? That's where I was the day before my birthday, sitting at a makeshift desk at the front of Forever 21, counting bodies walking in and out of the store for $10 an hour.

Ten dollars an hour. Hanging clothes, folding them, counting people as they came and went for 6-8 hours a day.

I couldn't stop thinking: *How did I end up here?*

I had a college degree. I had skills, talents, and a track record that proved I was capable of so much more. I had just spent months teaching in South Korea, navigating a foreign country during a global pandemic—an experience that pushed me to grow in ways I never thought possible.

And now? I was sitting there, counting bodies, wondering how I'd drifted so far off my path. It didn't make sense.

The truth is, I wasn't above the job. It was honest work, and I was grateful to have it. But deep down, I knew I was capable of so much more. Each person who walked through those doors wasn't just another tally—it was a reminder of where I was and where I knew I needed to be.

And then it hit me - that familiar voice of NO DOUBT rising up inside: "You're worth more than this. You know it. Now prove it."

The next day - my birthday - I walked in and quit. No backup plan. No safety net. Just pure, unwavering belief that I deserved more.

The 21-Day Revolution

Instead of celebrating my birthday with the usual festivities, I made a commitment to myself. For the next 21 days, I would:

- Wake up early
- Meditate
- Recite affirmations
- Study anything that could make me money

My new office? My mom's basement. My new coworkers? YouTube tutorials, motivational speakers and investment books. My new salary? Whatever I could manifest through pure hustle and determination.

The Crypto Chronicles

It was 2021, and something interesting was happening on Reddit. The r/WallStreetBets community was making waves, and I found myself diving deep into the comments, learning from strangers with usernames like "Bi66BootiesDroid11" (not financial advice, by the way). Every free moment was spent reading, studying, learning, analyzing.

Remember that deep work practice we talked about? This is where it really paid off. While others were randomly buying whatever coin was trending, I was:

- Studying market patterns
- Learning from past cycles
- Building systematic approaches
- Documenting everything

Then came Dogecoin. I got in at 0.003 (for my crypto investors out there, you know what that means). But the real game-changer came during a random late-night YouTube live group chat. It was around 4 AM, just eight strangers, talking about "Doge to the Moon!" That's when I first heard about SHIBA INU.

At the time, SHIBA was trading at 0.00000008. I threw $200 at it - about 2.5 billion SHIBA coins - and then, honestly, kind of forgot about it. But sometimes, the seeds you plant in moments of faith bloom when you least expect them to.

Through a combination of strategic moves and what felt like divine timing, I watched my initial $1,000 investment in stocks and crypto had grown to over $20,000 in a matter of months.

The Rise

Then came the real gains... The DogeCoin gains started small at first. A few hundred here, a thousand there. But then something magical started happening. My sister called a few months later, asking if I'd checked my SHIBA investment lately.

logged in, expecting to see the usual $221. Instead, I saw $4,000.
OMG! OMG!" I screamed. "What! What!" she yelled back. I could barely get the words out.

But that was just the beginning. The next few days were like a fever dream:

Monday: $5,201.98
Tuesday: $12,562
Wednesday: $27,936

Each day brought new highs, new possibilities. My mind started racing with dreams: "Lambo or Ferrari?" "LA, NYC, or Miami?" "How much are yachts these days?"

After about ten days, my account stabilized around $50K. I was still working with my first retainer design client, pulling in $4,800 a month, and now watching my crypto portfolio soar. Life was good. Actually, life was incredible. I was finally able to move out of my mom's basement into my first one bedroom apartment in downtown Grand Rapids, MI.

And then it happened - my account hit $100K.

Let me tell you something about seeing $100K in your account when you started with $200. It doesn't feel real. It's like you're living in someone else's story. I was floored. Bewildered. Stunned. Elated. Confused. All of it.

I had done it. I made it. I was financially free.

Or so I thought.

The Fall

It was a Saturday. I had invited some friends over to pregame before hitting the town. The vibe was good - drinks flowing, music playing, life feeling perfect. I was showing off my new Shiba NFT that I had just dropped $4,000 to mint.

Earlier, I'd noticed the NFT's image had changed, so I hopped into their Discord support chat to figure out what was up. An admin reached out to help, sending me a link to connect my account so they could resolve the issue.

Big mistake.

What happened next still plays in my mind like a slow-motion car crash. Password error. Input secret code. "Reconnect the API." All bullshit.

I refreshed my account. Zero balance in one coin. Refresh. Another zero. Refresh. Zero. Zero. Zero. I had broke the #1 rule of crypto trading.... NEVER give away your secret code.

"WTF IS GOING ON!!!! WHAT HAPPENED TO MY SHIT!"

But it was too late. The truth hit me like an anvil over my head. I got "got". Scammed out of $100K. Not $1 was left.

My friends could only watch in horror. "I'm sorry, bro." What else could they say? What else could anyone say?

"Is there anything you want us to do?"

I let out a defeated laugh. "Nah, I'm good. Wow... crazy.. I can't believe this.... You guys just go without me tonight, I'm gonna need a minute."

The Mindset Shift

In moments of crisis, we often turn to those who've lived long enough to have perspective. I called my grandma.

"Grandma... I'm so defeated. That was going to be my future! That was how I was gonna set myself up in a bigger city! I'm crushed! Like.... damnnn... whyyyyyyy?"

Her response changed everything. After a thoughtful sigh, she simply said, "Well Nicholas, I'm sorry for your loss. That's unfortunate, but your mindset about this whole thing is more impressive. Some people lose their hope over that kind of money loss, but I don't think you're defeated, just disappointed."

Then she asked me something profound: "How long did it take to make all that money?"

"Less than a year, a few months maybe?"
"Then you can make it back even faster next time and more of it, and now you know a valuable lesson."

In that moment, everything shifted. The loss was still there, but its meaning had changed. This wasn't the end of my story - it was just another chapter in my NO DOUBT journey.

The Real Lesson

Here's what I realized: They took my money, but they couldn't take what really mattered:

- The wisdom I'd gained
- The skills I'd developed
- The mindset I'd built
- The lessons I'd learned

So I did what any NO DOUBT warrior would do - I brushed myself off, cleaned myself up, and headed out to meet my boys. I was down, but I wasn't out.

The Transformation

Something crucial about the NO DOUBT mindset. It's not about:

- Never falling
- Never failing
- Never losing

It's about:

- How quickly you get back up
- What you learn from the fall
- Who you become in the process

Think about it - most people would've been destroyed by losing $100K. They would've:

- Given up on investing
- Blamed themselves endlessly
- Let it define their story
- Lost their confidence

But because of the foundation I was building (which we'll explore deeper in the coming chapter about what I call the Trifecta):

- My mind stayed strong

- My spirit stayed unbroken
- My vision stayed clear

The Real Value

Here's what most people don't understand about money: Your net worth isn't your self worth.

The true measure isn't in your bank account - it's in:

- Your ability to rebuild
- Your capacity to learn
- Your resilience under pressure
- Your unwavering belief in yourself

Now, I want you to think about your own setbacks. Maybe you haven't lost $100K in crypto, but we've all lost something that felt just as valuable at the time.

Ask yourself:

1. What skills or knowledge did you gain from that experience?
2. How did that setback make you stronger?
3. What would you do differently next time?
4. Most importantly, what would you do the same?

Remember, your circumstances don't define you - your response to them does. You can lose money, opportunities, even relationships, but no one can take away:

- Your growth
- Your knowledge
- Your NO DOUBT mindset

Building True Wealth: The NO DOUBT Way

Here's what losing $100K taught me about real wealth:

1. Knowledge Is Unloseable Currency

While the money vanished in seconds, no one could take:

- The market patterns I'd learned
- The analysis skills I'd developed
- The emotional control I'd mastered
- The strategic thinking I'd built

2. Speed of Recovery Matters More Than Speed of Success

It's not about:

- How fast you make it
- How much you make
- How impressive it looks

It's about:

- How fast you bounce back
- How well you learn

- How strong you become

3. The Foundation Principle

Your success can only be as strong as your foundation. That means:

- Mental preparation
- Emotional stability
- Strategic thinking
- Support system
- Daily disciplines

Moving Forward

Remember my grandmother's wisdom: "You can make it back even faster next time."

She was right, but not just about money. This applies to everything:

- Every setback makes you smarter
- Every loss makes you stronger
- Every fall makes you wiser

As long as you:

- Keep learning
- Stay humble
- Maintain discipline
- Trust the process

The Ultimate Truth

You're not defined by your bank balance, your worst mistakes, or your biggest losses. You're defined by your resilience, your growth, and your unwavering belief.

Because at the end of the day, true wealth isn't about having money - it's about having the power to create it again and again.

Let's get it.

Key Takeaways:

- Your net worth isn't your self worth
- Speed of recovery matters more than speed of success
- Knowledge is the only currency that can't be taken from you
- True wealth is the power to create value again and again

Your Turn:

1. Document your biggest setback and what it taught you
2. Map out your recovery strategy for future challenges
3. List the "unloseable" skills you've developed
4. Create your wealth-building foundation

What's Next: We'll discover how mind, body, and spirit work together to create unstoppable momentum.

7

Mind, Body, Spirit: The
Trifecta of Transformation

It's 5:43 AM. My arms shake as I lower myself for push-up number 491. The carpet beneath me is damp with sweat, every fiber of my being screaming to stop. But something deeper keeps me going.

This isn't just about physical strength. With each rep, I'm not just building muscle—I'm building mental fortitude. With each push-up, I'm not just challenging my body—I'm strengthening my spirit.

The Missing Link

Most people get this wrong. They fragment their focus, becoming living examples of imbalance. You've seen them—the gym rat with bulging muscles but scattered thoughts. The intellectual who can quote philosophers but can't touch their toes. The spiritual seeker who speaks of enlightenment but can't take decisive action.

I know because I've been all three. After leaving Forever 21, I realized something crucial: success isn't about developing one area—it's about integration.

The Wake-Up Call

Picture this: Day one of unemployment. I'm in my mom's basement, surrounded by personal development books, design tutorials, and a blank notebook. Coming from a job counting bodies at Forever 21, the contrast was stark. My mind brimmed with ambitious plans but lacked direction. My body had gone soft from years of sitting in cubicles. My spirit, once vibrant with possibility, had been drained by meaningless work.

Something had to change. Not just one thing - everything.

I committed to 21 days of total transformation. Not because it sounded good, but because I had no choice. Mediocrity had become more painful than the challenge ahead.

The Mind: Your Command Center

Day one began at 4:30 AM with nothing but silence and a blank notebook. No phone. No distractions. Just me and my thoughts. After years of following orders at my old 9-5, my mind needed to learn how to lead.

Remember that Rubik's Cube? It wasn't just about solving a puzzle. Each twist and turn was training my mind for deeper challenges ahead. Building the mental discipline to sit with complexity, to stay with problems long enough to crack them open.

The Body: Your Power Plant

Years of office chairs and comfort food had taken their toll. I was skinny, frail, always tired. The push-ups started as a desperate attempt to commit myself to SOMETHING. I needed to prove to myself I could keep going, even when it got hard.

The progression tells its own story.

- Week One: struggling to hit 50 reps, collapsing on the carpet, wondering if I was crazy.
- Week Two: breaking 200, starting to believe.
- Week Four: hitting 500, knowing I could never go back.
- Week Six: one thousand push-ups, understanding that my body's limits were mostly in my mind.

Every morning became a battle—not just against gravity, but against every voice saying, "stay in bed," "take it easy," "who are you trying to prove something to?" But with each rep, those voices got weaker. My body got stronger. My resolve hardened.

I developed what I call "Push-Up Psychology"—mental tricks that helped me break through barriers.

- "If you don't do one more, you won't be successful." Push-up 642.
- "Each rep is worth $1,000—how much money do you want to make in life?" Push-up 753.
- "Your future kids are watching—what example are you setting?" Push-up 891.

These weren't just motivational quotes. They were psychological triggers that linked my current pain to my future dreams. When my body wanted to quit, I created intense mental scenarios that made stopping feel more painful than continuing.

Crazy? Maybe. But this wasn't just about push-ups anymore. This was about building the kind of mind that could push through any barrier, face any challenge, overcome any obstacle. Because if I could convince myself to do another rep when my arms felt like jelly, what else could I convince myself to push through?

Each mental trick became a tool in my arsenal, proof that the mind could override the body's limits. These weren't just motivational quotes - they were psychological triggers that could instantly shift my state from exhaustion to determination.

I learned something powerful: Physical limitations are mostly mental barriers in disguise. The body can always do one more - it's the mind that needs convincing.

These mental games weren't just about push-ups - they were training for every challenge life would throw at me. Because once you learn to push through 'impossible' physical barriers, business challenges, creative blocks, and life obstacles don't stand a chance.

The Spirit: Finding Purpose Beyond the Paycheck

Before the push-ups, before opening a single book, I discovered something powerful in those pre-dawn hours: silence has a voice. Every morning, I'd sit in complete darkness, letting the stillness wash over me. Ten minutes to breathe. Ten minutes for gratitude. Ten minutes to envision who I was becoming.

Remember when we talked about knowing yourself? This is where that knowledge gets tested. In that morning silence, there's nowhere to hide from your truth. No social media to scroll through. No notifications to distract you. Just you, facing yourself in the dark, asking the questions that matter: What am I really here for? What am I willing to give everything for? What's the impact I'm meant to make?

The Integrated System

This transformation wasn't just about checking boxes or following someone else's routine. It was about creating a system that elevated every aspect of my life.

- **4:30 AM:** Cold water shock. Before doubt could creep in, I'd flood my mind with motivation—usually a powerful video or speech.
- **5:00 AM:** Pure silence. Breathing deeply, feeling my heartbeat, connecting with the fire inside.
- **5:30 AM:** Physical work begins. Each push-up becomes a declaration, building unshakable confidence.

- **6:30 AM:** Deep work. Studying, designing, building with no distractions. Three hours of focused effort worth more than an entire scattered day.

The magic wasn't in any single component—it was in how they fed each other. Physical strength fueled mental clarity. Mental focus enhanced spiritual connection. Spiritual purpose drove physical effort.

The Real Results

Within weeks, something remarkable started happening. The changes weren't just physical - though watching my push-up numbers climb was satisfying. They weren't just mental - though my ability to focus and solve problems had reached new levels. And they weren't just spiritual - though my sense of purpose had never been clearer.

The real transformation was in how these elements worked together. Design problems I would have struggled with for days now unfolded naturally during those focused morning hours. Client presentations that would have made me nervous now felt like opportunities to share energy. Every aspect of life began operating at a higher level.

Starting from zero in my mom's basement, I watched myself transform. My mind processed information faster, spotted opportunities others missed, made decisions with clarity I'd never known. My body hummed with energy that lasted all day, commanding presence in every room I entered. My spirit moved with a conviction that made doubt feel like a foreign concept.

The Hard Truth

Not every day was perfect. Some mornings, that 4:30 AM alarm felt like torture. Some days, the push-ups seemed impossible. But here's where most people get it wrong: when life threw curveballs, I didn't push it to tomorrow. Because tomorrow never comes. Every time you say "I'll do it tomorrow," you're really saying, "This isn't actually important to me."

But here's what separates those who break through from those who break down: The Trifecta isn't about perfection - it's about integration.

When your body's tired, you lean on mental strength.
When your mind's cloudy, you let your spirit guide.
When your spirit's low, you let physical movement energize you.

The only unacceptable option is quitting.

Making It Last

The secret to sustaining this isn't complicated, but it is demanding. Your first hour must be sacred - no compromises, no exceptions. Your physical training must progress - comfort is your enemy. Your spiritual practice must deepen - surface-level won't cut it.

This isn't about temporary change. It's about permanent transformation. Every morning, you're not just working out - you're working on becoming someone who can't be stopped. Every meditation isn't just about finding peace - it's about finding power. Every moment of deep work isn't just about getting things done - it's about bringing your vision to life.

Your mind won't stay sharp without a strong body to support it. Your body won't push through limits without spiritual purpose driving it. Your spirit needs a clear mind to direct its energy. This is what makes the Trifecta unbeatable.

The system works because it's complete. It addresses every aspect of who you are and who you're becoming. It transforms not just what you do, but who you are.

Not just your habits, but your identity.

This is how you become unstoppable.

Key Takeaways:

- True transformation requires mind, body, and spirit integration
- The first hour of your day determines everything that follows
- Consistency matters more than perfection
- Real power comes from the synergy of all three elements

Your Turn:

- 1. Design your morning power hour
- 2. Start your physical practice (even if it's just 10 push-ups)
- 3. Create your spiritual practice
- 4. Build your integration system

What's Next: We'll examine how your circle of influence shapes your destiny.

8

The Circle Audit: Friends or Liabilities?

You're About to Hate Me

Because I'm about to tell you something that's going to hurt. Something that might make you angry, defensive, or want to put this book down. But I need you to hear it, because this might be the most important chapter in this entire book.

Your friends are killing your dreams.

Not all of them. But enough of them. And deep down, you already know this.

THE WAKE-UP CALL

Let me tell you about one of the hardest conversations I've ever had.

It was after implementing my morning routine, after starting to see real changes in my life. I was beginning to transform, but something was holding me back. Or rather, someone.

My best friend and I were living what we thought was the life. We'd go out, grab drinks, stay out late. We'd laugh, drink, and try to talk to as many girls as we could. Classic twentysomething stuff, right?

Wrong.

We were ignoring our problems, living for cheap thrills, and running from our potential.

Here's the thing about my best friend—he had gifts, talents, and capabilities that he couldn't see in himself. And it was breaking my heart to watch us squander that potential night after night. I knew he could be more. Hell, I knew we could be more.

The Conversation That Changed Everything

So one day, I did something that terrified me. I sat him down for a conversation that would either end our friendship or transform it.

"Look," I said, "you're my best friend, and I want to keep you in my life. But I'm going through something personal, and I need to make a change. I'd like you to be there with me, but I can't slow down, and I'm not waiting for you. I hope you understand, but I really need you to get your shit together. I'd hate to have to do this without you, but I will if I have to. This is important to me, and you're important to me."

Silence. The kind that feels like forever.

He didn't take it well at first. He felt like I was saying I was too good for him, that he wasn't enough because he was still in school and hadn't graduated yet. We yelled. We argued. But I had to be honest with myself and where I was going.

A week later, my phone rang.

"Hey," he said, "I just want to thank you. Nobody has ever talked to me that way. Not my mom, not my grandparents, not my friends. Nobody has told me that I could be doing more with my life and that I was missing out on being the better version of myself."

The Result

Today, as you're reading this book, he's graduated. He's holding down a cushy job as an engineer at a major manufacturing company. He's got a beautiful wife and two lovely children. We still talk about that moment and how it altered our life.

This story isn't just about friendship. It's about understanding a crucial truth:

Sometimes being a real friend means being willing to risk the friendship itself for the other person's growth.

THE THREE FRIENDS YOU ACTUALLY NEED

1. *The Challenger*

This is someone who:

- Calls you out on your BS
- Pushes you to think bigger
- Holds you accountable
- Celebrates your wins but never lets you get comfortable

Like my first art professor at Hampton who first noticed my art & design abilities and said, "You're very good at this. Why aren't you doing more with it?" He pushed me to embrace my authentic self.

2. *The Growth Partner*

Someone who:

- Is actively working on themselves
- Shares resources and opportunities
- Discusses ideas, not people
- Matches your energy for improvement

Remember my coworker who tracked my Rubik's Cube progress? That's a growth partner. They're invested in your development.

3. *The Success Model*

Someone who:

- Is where you want to be
- Proves what's possible
- Shares real insights
- Lives what they preach

These people might not be your closest friends, but they show you what's possible. If you don't know anyone personally, reach out to someone you admire on social media. You never know what could happen by simply reaching out. You know the saying, "closed mouths don't get fed."

Here's a sample message you can use to reach out:

"*Hi [Name],*

I hope you're doing great! I've been following your journey, and I just wanted to say how much I admire your work and the way you [specific detail, e.g., "bring creativity and authenticity to everything you do"]. It's so inspiring to see someone who [specific aspect, e.g., "is achieving their goals while staying true to themselves"].

I'm curious—what's one piece of advice you'd give to someone trying to [specific goal, e.g., "break into this industry" or "stay consistent while building something meaningful"]?

Thank you for sharing so much value and inspiration. I'd love to hear your thoughts if you have a moment.

Best,

Your Name"

Let's get something straight right now—your circle isn't about quantity. It's about quality.

Now, look at your phone. Open your recent calls and messages. How many of these three types of friends do you have? Be honest.

Most people have none. What they have instead are:

The Comfort Friends
- Keep you in your comfort zone
- "Just be happy with what you have"
- Never challenge you to grow
- Enable your old patterns

The Fun Friends
- Great for a good time
- Terrible for growth
- Always there for parties
- Nowhere to be found during struggles

The Toxic Friends
- "Everything happens for a reason!"
- Never address real issues
- Only talk about drama
- Avoid hard conversations

The Dream Killers
- Call it "being realistic"
- Point out every possible failure
- Share horror stories of others who tried
- Keep you playing small

And here's where it gets uncomfortable: Some of your "day ones" might be holding you back.

The Power of Real Transformation

Let me tell you about Michael. When I first met him, he was impossible to miss—long blonde hair flowing to his shoulders, gold chains, and rings catching the light, and a sense of style that was completely his own. Another creative soul, we connected instantly. We used to do everything together—chasing girls, riding dirt bikes, and throwing parties all the time. Life was a blur of adrenaline and distractions, and for a while, it felt like nothing could touch us.

But then something shifted. When I started to change—when I began focusing on my grind, my hustle, those early mornings and late nights—Michael noticed. He watched when I'd disappear for days to focus on my craft. He saw the shift in my priorities, the way I stopped chasing temporary highs and started building something real.

At first, he was living like most of us do—chasing the image, drowning in distractions, trying to fit the mold others had created for him. But something was stirring beneath the surface.

Then one day, he'd had enough. Enough of the surface-level success. Enough of the material masks. Enough of playing small.

That's when something changed. He didn't just adopt the NO DOUBT mindset—he embodied it. Stripped away everything that wasn't serving his growth. Started building his own agency. Got married. Then made a move that shocked everyone—packed up and relocated to Montana to become a creative director at bad ass luxury boat dealership.

But here's the thing about real transformation—it's not about the external changes. It's about who you become in the process. Now Michael's up before dawn, hitting the gym, building systems, and expanding his impact. No more late nights at the club, no more chasing temporary highs. **He's building legacy.**

And the most powerful part? His transformation isn't just about him anymore. People around him are noticing. They see the change, feel the energy, and want what he's found. **That's the real power of NO DOUBT**—when one person steps into their truth, they give others permission to do the same.

Michael's story isn't just about personal success. It's about what happens when you stop doubting and start becoming. When you trade surface-level validation for deep, authentic power. When you choose growth over comfort.

Because real transformation isn't about changing who you are—it's about becoming who you were always meant to be.

Now that you've seen what real transformation looks like, it's time to look at your own circle.

Let's do the work.

The Audit Process

Time for some real work. Grab your phone and a notebook. We're about to do something that might hurt, but it's necessary.

For each person in your close circle, answer these questions:

1. When was the last time they pushed you to be better?
2. Do they make you feel energized or drained after hanging out?
3. Have they grown in the last year, or are they the same person?
4. Would they support a major life change, or try to talk you out of it?
5. Do they represent who you want to be, or who you used to be?

Breaking Down Your Circle

Let me show you exactly how this played out in my life. After doing this audit, I realized something shocking:

80% of my interactions were with people who were:

- Focused on past memories
- Living for the weekend

- Making excuses for mediocrity
- Afraid of real change

No wonder I felt stuck. I was surrounding myself with stuck people.

Building Your New Circle

Let me be clear: This isn't about cutting everyone off. It's about being strategic with your time and energy. Here's how I rebuilt my circle:

Step 1: The Time Audit

Track where your time goes for one week:

- Who do you talk to most?
- What do you talk about?
- How do you feel after?

I did this after that conversation with my best friend and realized I was spending 20+ hours a week in environments that weren't serving my growth.

Step 2: Strategic Positioning

Start putting yourself in places where growth-minded people gather:

- Morning gym sessions (serious people train early)
- Skills workshops

- Industry Conferences
- Professional meetups
- Places where your future circle hangs out

During my design journey, I started attending creative meetups. Not to sell anything, but to be around people who were serious about their craft.

Step 3: The Value-First Approach

Here's what most people get wrong – they try to network by taking. Instead:

- Share what you're learning
- Offer genuine help
- Connect others
- Add value before asking for anything

Remember: Quality relationships aren't built in a day. They're built through consistent, valuable interactions.

Handling the Pushback

Let me tell you what's about to happen when you start making these changes:

The Guilt Trips

- "You think you're better than us now?"

- "You've changed"
- "Remember when you used to be fun?"
- "Why are you acting brand new?"

When I started waking up at 4:30 AM and skipping late-night hang-outs, the comments came quick: "Oh, look at Mr. Motivated." "Since when are you too good for us?"

The Pull Back

People will try to drag you back to their level:

- Last-minute invites to throw off your routine
- Subtle jabs at your new habits
- Reminders of past failures
- Attempts to make you doubt yourself

The Real Talk

Here's the truth: Some people would rather see you stay the same than watch you outgrow them. Your growth is a mirror they're not ready to look into.

Remember when my best friend initially got defensive? He wasn't really mad at me – he was confronting his own reflection.

How to Handle It

Be Firm, but Kind

- Explain your goals
- Invite them to grow with you
- Set clear boundaries
- Stick to your standards

Create Distance Gradually

- Reduce exposure slowly
- Maintain respect
- Keep doors open for those who might catch up
- Focus on your growth

Fill the Void

- Replace old habits with new ones
- Build new connections
- Create growth-focused routines
- Invest in yourself

Remember what my grandmother told me after I lost everything in crypto? She said I could build it back faster because I had the knowledge and experience.

The same is true for your circle. Yes, it might feel hard to let go of old friends. Yes, it might be uncomfortable to put yourself out there. Yes, you might feel lonely sometimes.

But here's what I know:

The temporary discomfort of growth is nothing compared to the permanent pain of staying the same.

Your circle is your ceiling. Your friends are your future. Your relationships are your net worth.

Choose wisely.

Let's get it.

Key Takeaways:

- Your circle determines your ceiling
- Real friendship sometimes means risking the friendship for growth
- Quality of relationships matters more than quantity
- Growth often requires strategic distance from old patterns

Your Turn:

1. Complete your circle audit (who's helping vs. holding?) - Take 5 minutes right now to write down names - Be brutally honest with yourself - Note your immediate emotional response to each name 2. Identify your three essential relationships 3. Create your strategic positioning plan 4. Practice the firm-but-kind approach

What's Next: Discover how to turn your creative gifts into unstoppable momentum.

PART III: BUILDING THE FOUNDATION

Once you've broken through, the next step is to create stability—a foundation strong enough to support everything you're building. Without it, success becomes fragile and fleeting. But with it, you can create a life of purpose and impact that lasts.

In these chapters, you'll discover how to take your vision and turn it into reality through structure, systems, and discipline. This is where strategy meets action, where big ideas are transformed into tangible outcomes.

What kind of life do you want to build—one that crumbles under pressure or one that stands the test of time? The tools and principles I'll share helped me shift from merely surviving to thriving, and they can do the same for you.

This isn't just about achieving goals; it's about becoming the kind of person who can handle success with clarity, confidence, and consistency. The foundation you build now will determine the heights you can reach.

So, let's make it solid.

9

The Creator's Code: Turning Ideas into Reality

Picture this: I'm sitting in my mom's basement at 2 AM, staring at my first real client proposal. The project? A pitch deck design. My finger hovers over the "Send" button as doubt floods my mind.

"Who am I to charge $1,500 for this?"

But something deeper whispers: "Who are you not to?"

I close my eyes, take a deep breath, and hit send.

Three days later, the client uses that deck to raise $50,000 in funding. A month later, they refer me to another company that becomes a $5,000/month retainer.

That's when it hit me: I wasn't selling design. I was selling transformation.

Here's what most creators never realize: *Your worth isn't in your time—it's in the change you create.*

Think about it:

- A logo isn't just graphics—it's the cornerstone of a business's identity.
- A website isn't just code—it's a revenue-generating machine that works 24/7.
- A design isn't just aesthetics—it's the bridge between what is and what could be.

But most creators stay trapped:

- Charging hourly when they should be charging for impact.
- Competing on price when they should be competing on value.
- Playing small when they should be transforming lives.

Let me show you how to break free.

The Three Levels of Value

Level 1: Execution

This is where most people stay—focusing on deliverables, competing on price, measuring success by completion. I know because I lived here, designing car ads for $10 an hour, dying inside with each generic template. Every project felt like another piece of my soul fading away.

Level 2: Solution

This is where you start solving real problems. That first pitch deck? It wasn't about the slides—it was about helping a business secure their future. When you shift from making things to solving problems, everything changes.

Level 3: Transformation

This is where magic happens. Remember that client who raised $50K? Their success wasn't just about the money—it was about proving what's possible. Six months later, they came back with a $15,000 project. Not because I got better at design, but because they saw me as a partner in their growth.

The Transformation Framework

1. Ask Power Questions

- Instead of: "What do you need?"
  Ask: "What transformation are you seeking?"
- Instead of: "When do you need it?"
  Ask: "What's driving this timing?"
- Instead of: "What's your budget?"
  Ask: "What would achieving this goal be worth to your business?"

2. Build Value Packages

Foundation Level: ($1,000+)

- Core brand elements
- Implementation strategy

- Success roadmap

Growth Level: ($5,000-10,000/month)

- Strategic direction
- Ongoing evolution
- Business integration
- ROI tracking

Authority Level: ($20,000+)

- Market positioning
- Category dominance
- Business transformation
- Legacy building

3. Create Systems That Scale

When I started getting serious clients, I was drowning—60-hour weeks, constant stress, endless revisions. Then I built what I call the Creation Framework:

- Clear processes that eliminate chaos
- Templates that maintain excellence
- Systems that multiply impact
- Frameworks that scale value

Result? My work hours dropped by 80%. My income quadrupled. But most importantly? My impact deepened.

The Real Secret

Here's what transformed everything: Stop seeing yourself as a service provider. Start seeing yourself as a catalyst for change.

Your creativity isn't just a skill—it's a force for transformation. Your designs aren't just deliverables—they're bridges to possibility. Your work isn't just a job—it's a vehicle for impact.

Remember that kid in the basement, scared to charge $1,500? He didn't know that two years later, he'd be closing five-figure deals. Not because he got better at design—because he understood his real value.

The Path Forward

Here's your exact next steps:

1. **This Week**

   Choose one project. Don't just deliver it—transform it. Show your client not just what you can make, but what you can change.

2. **This Month**

   Document your processes. Build your value packages. Start asking power questions.

3. **This Quarter**

   Scale your systems. Raise your rates. Deepen your impact.

Your creativity is a gift. Your vision is valuable. Your work can transform lives.

Stop playing small. Start creating change.

Let's get it.

Key Takeaways:

- Value lives in transformation, not time.
- Systems enable impact without burnout.
- Your creativity is worth more than you think.
- Change starts with how you see yourself.

Your Next Action:

Review your current projects right now. For each one, ask: "What transformation am I really selling?" Let your answer guide everything that follows.

10

The Power of Preparation: The Hidden Edge

"Good morning, Mr. Alexander! How was your flight? I saw your talk at SXSW last month about Netflix's approach to creative freedom - brilliant insights about the future of content."

The look on his face was priceless. Here I was, just a volunteer at a top NYC design conference, and I'd stopped a Netflix VP in his tracks. What followed wasn't just a conversation - it was fifteen minutes that would change the trajectory of my career.

But this wasn't luck. This wasn't chance. And it definitely wasn't just charm.

This was preparation meeting opportunity.

Let me tell you the real story - the one that happened long before that moment. Because while most people focus on the big breaks, the lucky chances, the "right place, right time" moments, I'm going to show you what actually creates those moments.

Picture this: 9:20 AM, I'm speed-walking into the office, already 20 minutes late, coffee in hand, preparing my usual excuse about traffic. Another day of designing car advertisements. Another day of feeling my creativity slowly die.

But something was different this morning. Maybe it was the Gary Vee podcast I'd been listening to on the drive in. Maybe it was watching another friend get promoted while I stayed stagnant. Or maybe it was just that voice - that NO DOUBT voice - finally getting loud enough to drown out my excuses.

"What if you treated this job like it was your dream job?"

The thought stopped me in my tracks. Right there in the parking lot.

This is where most people get it wrong. They wait for the perfect opportunity before giving their full effort. They wait for the dream job before bringing their A-game. They wait for permission to be great.

But real transformation? It starts long before the opportunity arrives.

The Experiment

Instead of dragging myself through another day, I decided to run an experiment. Not just about showing up early or working harder - but about preparation as a competitive advantage.

The changes started small: 8:45 AM arrival instead of 9:20. Grant Cardone's "10X Rule" replaced random Spotify playlists. Lunch breaks became YouTube study sessions instead of Netflix binges. Every moment became an investment in what could be, not just an escape from what was.

But here's what most people miss about preparation: It's not just about doing more. It's about seeing more. While everyone else saw limitations, I started seeing possibilities.

The Real Work

Living at my dad's house at the time, I was saving for what I thought would be my escape to California. Classic story, right? Small-town designer dreams of making it big on the West Coast. Every night, scrolling through apartment listings, planning my grand exit.

Then one evening, my dad walks in. Instead of the usual "When are you moving out?" conversation I was expecting, he offers something different:

"You know, instead of paying me rent, why don't you invest that money into some conferences? Connect with other designers? If you're not satisfied here, maybe see what else is out there?"

I stopped scrolling. Something clicked.

See, this wasn't just about saving money. This was about investing in myself. All those mornings listening to Gary Vee and Grant Cardone suddenly made sense.

They weren't just talking about hustling - they were talking about strategic positioning.

And that night, everything shifted. Instead of scrolling through apartments I couldn't afford, I dove deep into research mode:

- Design conferences worldwide
- Speaker lineups
- Past attendee reviews
- Career impact stories

Then I found it. The Adobe 99U Conference in New York City. This wasn't just another conference. This was where creative directors shared their visions, where industry leaders revealed their playbooks, where global brands showcased what was next. This was where careers weren't just advanced - they were transformed. This was the epicenter of what was possible in design.

The name itself had meaning - inspired by Thomas Edison's belief that genius is 1% inspiration and 99% perspiration. This wasn't about theory or surface-level inspiration. This was about the real work, the deep insights, the kind of knowledge that could transform a designer's career from good to extraordinary.

Reading through the speaker list felt like scanning the credits of every major design project I'd ever admired. Nike. Netflix. Disney. We-Work. Behance. Dropbox. The giants of creative industry, all in one place.

Only two problems stood in my way:

Tickets: $1,000
Location: New York City

Total cost with travel and accommodation? Way more than I had. Way more than I could save. Way more than seemed possible.

For about 30 seconds, I felt that familiar sinking feeling. You know the one—when reality crashes into dreams and dreams usually lose.

But then that NO DOUBT voice kicked in. The same voice that got me to work early. The same voice that replaced music with education. The same voice that kept saying, *"there's more out there."*

"If there's a will, there's a way. Find the way, Nick."

So I kept scrolling. Kept reading. Kept looking for the opportunity hidden in the obstacle. And there it was, buried at the bottom of the page:

"Volunteer Applications Now Open."

Those words that would change everything. I applied that same night, pouring everything I had into that application, and three days later, I got the email that made me shout out loud. Not only had I been accepted as a volunteer, but I had been selected as a **Lead Volunteer** and assigned to the **VIP table!**

Theee VIP table. The place where every speaker and every big name would check in. The place I was supposed to manage.

In that moment, the dream that once seemed impossible didn't just feel possible—it felt inevitable.

The Preparation System

Now, here's where most people mess up. They see an opportunity, they take a shot, and then they wait. Hope becomes their strategy. But hope isn't a strategy - preparation is.

I had 5 weeks until the conference. That meant 5 weeks to turn myself into the most prepared volunteer in conference history. This wasn't just about showing up - this was about showing up ready to create impact.

My schedule became my weapon:

Morning (Before Work):

6:00 AM: Research one speaker's background
6:30 AM: Study their company's latest projects
7:00 AM: Watch their previous talks
7:30 AM: Take detailed notes

Lunch Break:

- Industry interviews
- Company strategies
- Future predictions
- Market trends

Evening:

- Create speaker dossiers
- Map out conference schedule
- Plan strategic conversations
- Identify key networking moments

By the time the conference came around, I didn't just know these speakers' names - I knew their career paths, their company strategies, their creative philosophies, their recent projects, even which ones had dogs and what they named them.

Too much? Maybe. But that's what preparation looks like when you're serious about creating opportunity, not just waiting for it.

Game Day

7:30 AM, New York City. I'm standing outside the conference venue while the city's still waking up. Other volunteers are trickling in, coffee cups in hand, looking half-asleep. But I'm wide awake. This isn't just another day - this is everything I've been preparing for.

The volunteer coordinator gathers us for orientation: "Remember, you're here to help. Don't bother the speakers about jobs or opportunities."

I smile to myself. I wasn't here to ask for jobs. I was here to make an impression.

At the VIP Welcome Desk - the exact position I wanted to be - every moment of preparation started paying off. As each speaker arrived:

"Good morning, Mr. Johnson! How was your flight from San Francisco?"
"Ms. Rodriguez! Loved your recent piece on creative leadership."
"Mr. Patel! That WeWork campaign was brilliant!"
The looks on their faces - priceless. You could see them wondering, "How does this volunteer know all this?"

Other volunteers started noticing: "Yo, do you know everyone here?" "How do you remember all this?" "Did you work with them before?"
My response? "Nope. I just did my homework."

The Moment Everything Changed

Then came the moment all that preparation was building toward. During a lunch break, I spot him - the VP from Netflix I'd studied extensively. He's walking past the welcome desk, checking his phone.

Remember all those early mornings watching his talks? Time to put that knowledge to work.

"Excuse me, sir. Really enjoyed your talk at SXSW about Netflix's approach to creative freedom. Is it true what they're saying about Netflix planning to open theaters?"

He stops. Looks up from his phone. Smiles.

What was supposed to be a quick question turned into a fifteen-minute conversation about the future of streaming, creative direction, content strategy, and industry evolution. His colleague joins in, fascinated by the depth of the conversation.

The other volunteers are stunned: "What just happened?"

But here's what they didn't see:

- The 5 AM study sessions
- The pages of notes
- The hours of research
- The preparation that made this "lucky" moment possible

The Ripple Effect

But this isn't just about impressing executives at conferences. This level of preparation changes everything. Let me show you exactly how this played out.

During a break, the volunteer coordinator pulled me aside: "Nick, I don't know what it is about you, but you've got something special. The way you handle the speakers, your attention to detail, your enthusiasm... Would you be interested in working another Adobe event?"

"Absolutely!"

"Great. We've got one coming up in July in San Francisco. Paid position this time. $25 an hour, 12-14 hour days. Plus, you will get a chance to visit the Adobe SF building!"

Do the math: In four days, I could make more than half my monthly salary at the media company. But the money wasn't even the best part. This was validation.

This was proof that preparation creates opportunities that luck never could.

The Preparation Principle

Let me break down exactly what makes this work, because this goes way beyond conferences:

1. Research Becomes Your Superpower

- Want to land a dream client? Study their business like you're already part of their team
- Want to get hired? Know more about the company than their current employees
- Want to stand out in your industry? Become a student of what's next, not just what's now

2. Details Create Distinction

- While others know names, you know stories
- While others see surface, you understand depth
- While others wait for instruction, you anticipate needs

3. Value Comes Before Opportunity

- Don't wait to be asked - be ready to contribute
- Don't wait for positions to open - create roles through value
- Don't wait for permission - prepare for possibility

The Universal Application

Let me show you exactly how this works in any field:

For Creators: Before you pitch that client - study their entire brand history, know their competitors, understand their market position. When you walk in with solutions to problems they haven't even voiced yet, you're not just another vendor - you're a strategic partner.

For Job Seekers: Before that dream interview - know every project the company has launched in the last year, understand their challenges, have ideas ready for their future. When you can discuss their business like an insider, you're not just another candidate - you're a valuable asset.

For Entrepreneurs: Before you launch that business - deeply understand your market, know your competitors' every move, see the gaps no one else has noticed.

When you can spot opportunities others miss, you're not just starting a business - you're solving a real need.

The Preparation Framework

Here's exactly how to apply this in your life:

1. Deep Research Phase

- Go beyond Google
- Study patterns and trends
- Understand context
- Map out connections

2. Strategic Analysis

- Identify opportunities
- Spot potential challenges
- Prepare specific solutions
- Build unique insights

3. Value Creation

- Develop actionable ideas
- Create useful insights
- Build valuable connections
- Position for impact

Real World Results

Let me show you this framework in action:

A Designer's Story: Before pitching a $20K branding project, she spent two weeks studying the client's entire 10-year history. In the meeting, she shocked them by pointing out brand inconsistencies they hadn't noticed. Result? She won the project over agencies triple her size.

A Developer's Edge: Instead of just applying to tech companies, he spent months contributing to their open-source projects. By the time he interviewed, he knew their codebase better than some employees. He had job offers from three major companies.

A Photographer's Breakthrough: Before pitching a major fashion brand, she studied every campaign they'd run for five years. She identified a visual pattern they'd abandoned that had produced their best results. They hired her to revive it.

This is what all breakthrough performers have in common - across every field, every industry, every era. Look at the greats:

Kobe Bryant's preparation was legendary. While others saw him sinking game-winning shots, they didn't see him arriving at 4 AM to shoot 2,000 baskets every morning. He didn't just practice - he studied every opponent's tendencies, their breathing patterns, their dominant hand movements, even their preferred escape routes on defense. When teammates would arrive for 11 AM practice, they'd find him drenched in sweat, having already put in a full day's work. In crucial moments, what looked like natural talent to observers was actually thousands of hours of preparation meeting opportunity.

Sara Blakely, the founder of Spanx, spent two years preparing and researching while working her day job selling fax machines. She didn't just have an idea - she studied every patent in hosiery, wrote her own patent to save legal fees, pitched to manufacturers until she found one who believed in her vision, and tested countless prototypes herself. She prepared so thoroughly that when she finally got her meeting with Neiman Marcus, she was ready to demonstrate her product in the bathroom to prove its effectiveness. That's how a former fax machine saleswoman became the youngest self-made female billionaire - not through luck, but through relentless preparation.

Christopher Nolan takes preparation in filmmaking to another level entirely. Before shooting begins, he spends years preparing for each film. He doesn't just write scripts - he draws every single shot by hand, creates detailed notebooks filled with research and references, and builds elaborate timelines to track complex storylines. For "Inception," he spent nearly a decade developing the idea, studying dreams, and creating rules for his universe before filming a single scene. When other directors marvel at his complex shots, they're really marveling at years of preparation made visible.

The same principle applies to your field:

- Athletes study film, you study your market
- Entrepreneurs test products, you test ideas
- Directors plan shots, you plan moves
- Every master prepares for breakthroughs

The Common Thread:

- They don't wait for opportunities
- They create leverage through knowledge
- They solve problems before being asked
- They position themselves as invaluable

The difference between good and great isn't just talent - it's the depth of preparation. While others rely on natural ability, the greats understand that preparation creates possibilities that talent alone never could.

The Universal Law of Preparation

Look at what these masters have in common:

1. They Prepare Deeper Than Required

- Kobe didn't just practice shots - he studied breathing patterns
- Sara didn't just design a product - she mastered patent law
- Nolan doesn't just write scenes - he draws every single shot

2. They Focus on What Others Ignore

- While others practice the obvious, they study the subtle
- While others chase shortcuts, they build foundations
- While others wait for chances, they create certainty

3. They Make Preparation Their Competitive Edge

- It's not about natural talent
- It's not about luck
- It's not about being in the right place
- It's about being ready when opportunity appears

Creating Inevitable Success

Here's what happens when you adopt this level of preparation:

1. You Stop Competing and Start Creating

Instead of wondering if you're good enough, you know you're ready. When others are hoping for their shot, you're creating your breakthrough.

2. Opportunities Multiple

What looks like "lucky breaks" to others become inevitable outcomes of your preparation. The more prepared you are, the more opportunities you seem to "attract."

3. Fear Transforms into Fuel

When you're thoroughly prepared:

- Pressure becomes performance
- Challenges become chances
- Big moments become proving grounds

Because here's the truth: Success isn't about hoping you're ready when opportunity knocks. It's about being so prepared that opportunity breaks down your door. The preparation mindset says:

- There are no lucky breaks, only prepared moments
- There are no overnight successes, only unseen preparation
- There are no natural talents, only dedicated preparation

The Final Truth

The world doesn't reward people who wait for their moment. It rewards those who prepare like their life depends on it. Because in reality, your future does depend on it.

Every morning when that alarm goes off, you have a choice:

- Hit snooze like everyone else, or
- Start preparing like the greats

Every free moment presents the same decision:

- Scroll mindlessly like the masses, or
- Study purposefully like the masters

Every day asks the same question:

- Are you hoping for success?
- Or are you ensuring it?

Remember: Luck is what people call preparation when they don't see the work behind it.

So prepare like Kobe at 4 AM. Study like Sara with those patents. Plan like Nolan with those notebooks.

Because when preparation becomes who you are, success becomes what you do.

Let's get it.

Key Takeaways:

- Success isn't about luck - it's about preparation meeting opportunity
- Real preparation is about depth, not just time invested
- Small, consistent preparation compounds into massive advantages
- When you're truly prepared, opportunities find you

Your Turn:

1. Choose one area where you'll become the most prepared person in the room
2. Create your daily preparation system
3. Start building your knowledge base
4. Turn preparation into your competitive edge

What's Next: We'll explore how to turn your skills into a global breakthrough.

11

The Korea Chronicles: NO DOUBT in Action

1 PM. Incheon Airport has gone dark. I'm standing on a street corner surrounded by three oversized suitcases and a bulging backpack, watching my taxi driver disappear into the night after charging me $150 for a $30 ride. Rookie mistake #1.

I forgot to tell my phone carrier I was going to be abroad and would need service. So you know what that means…

No phone service.
No way to contact my employer.
No ability to read a single sign.

And absolutely no way to know if I'm even in the right neighborhood. Welcome to the ultimate NO DOUBT test.

You know those moments that reveal exactly what you're made of? When all your preparation, all your systems, all your confidence gets put to the real test? This wasn't just one of those moments - this was preparation meeting reality at full speed.

Most people would panic. Hell, part of me wanted to. But here's what most people don't understand about preparation: It's not just about having a plan - it's about having the clarity to think when everything goes wrong.

Through the neon blur of signs I couldn't read, I spot something familiar: a cell phone store, still lit up despite the hour. Dragging my life behind me like a one-man caravan, I approach with what I hope is a universal "please help me" smile.

Ten minutes and many charades later, I'm able to contact my employer. First crisis averted. But the night was just beginning.

She leads me to my new home - a tiny studio apartment about the size of a standard dorm room that would become both sanctuary and testing ground. She demonstrates the door code, I punch it in successfully, and she leaves. Simple enough.

Still needing WiFi for my phone, another teacher offers to show me around the neighborhood. Nothing's open this late, but at least I'm starting to get my bearings. Exhausted, I head back to my apartment, ready to finally crash.

91351... "Come on." ERROR.

Try again...

"Fuuuuckk..." DENIED

It's 1 AM, and I'm officially locked out. Everything I own - my clothes, toiletries, my entire life - sits just on the other side of this door, taunting me through a few inches of steel.

My employer comes through with a temporary solution: access to an empty room under maintenance next door. No working lights. No plumbing. Just a plastic-wrapped mattress on the ground.

My world has been reduced to:

- My NO DOUBT APPAREL TM fanny pack
- A phone with no service
- Some airplane peanuts
- A travel pack of Starbursts
- A neck pillow
- And a decision

Standing in that dark room, staring at that plastic mattress, I could either break down or find the humor. That's when it hit me - this laugh bubbling up from somewhere deep inside.

"Whelp!! HAHAHAHAHAHAHA!!! Welcome to SOUTH KO-REA, my boy!!"

That laugh in the darkness wasn't just amusement. It was recognition. Every challenge either breaks you or builds you. I chose to let it build me.

After a few hours of uncomfortable sleep, I woke with determination burning in my chest. Twenty minutes of pacing the halls, holding my phone in the air like Simba in The Lion King - but instead of presenting the future king, I'm begging for one bar of WiFi. The other teachers suggest waiting for maintenance to reset the code, but it's Sunday. So they won't be back until Monday.

Standing in that hallway, staring at that keypad for what felt like the hundredth time, something clicks. All those numbers... all those combinations... what if...

My fingers hover over the keypad. One last try before admitting defeat.

This time, I switch the last two numbers around.
beep
Green light.
The door clicks open.

I let out an exhausted maniacal laugh that echoes through the hallway. That feeling of victory - of figuring something out when everything seems impossible - that's what NO DOUBT is all about. But this was just the beginning.

Because surviving that first night wasn't enough. I needed WiFi to function in this new world. And getting it would mean navigating the

Seoul subway system - thirty stops across a city where I couldn't read a single sign.

Think about that for a moment. Picture navigating New York's subway system for the first time. Now imagine doing it in a city where you can't read a single sign, can't ask for directions, and your destination is thirty stops away.

Most people would have waited for help. Stayed safe. Played small.

But that's not what we're here to do.

The Subway Strategy

First step: Get to the station. I hail a cab, point to the subway station on my phone. Basic enough.

Second step: Staring at the napkin notes my co-teacher had scribbled down the night before at a local cafe. The city names blurred together through my jet-lagged eyes. After 14 hours of flying, every station name looked identical. Not exactly confidence inspiring, but it was all I had.

I walk up to the ticket counter with my best "which direction to...?" face - you know the one, eyebrows raised, pointing vaguely in multiple directions while holding up my phone with "Airport" displayed. She nods, points to a number. I bow in thanks - at least I knew that part.

Thirty stops. Each one a mix of hope and anxiety. Each station name a blur in my exhausted state. But with each successful station, my confidence grows a little.

Two hours later, I'm walking out of the airport with a portable WiFi router in my hand, feeling like I just conquered the world. Not because I had any real idea what I was doing, but because sometimes the bravest thing you can do is just start moving and trust that you'll figure it out along the way.

But here's what I didn't know then - this wasn't just about getting WiFi. This was about proving something crucial:

When you strip away all your normal tools... When you can't rely on language... When all you've got is a jet-lagged brain and a napkin full of station names you can barely read... That's when you discover what you're really made of.

Here's what I posted on Facebook after that adventure:

"March 3, 2020
I must say... I'm pretty damn proud of myself right now. After a rough first night, I completed my first big mission on my own here in South Korea.
I needed to get some WiFi so I could keep in touch with my friends and family (and basically everything else). But that meant taking the subway across the city - thirty stops - to an airport to find a kiosk that sold portable WiFi routers specifically for foreigners.

I remember when using the New York subway system was intimidating and scary for me. But I'm proud to say... 'MISSION ACCOMPLISHED'

I hailed a cab to the nearest subway stop. Asked the subway teller which way to the airport (no English mind you, all just sign language and assumptions) and hopped on the train hoping I'm going the right way... rode it all the way to my destination and found my way to the right kiosk. Bought my router and now I'm headed home.

I'm writing this on the subway now, but I just want to say that if there is a will.. there IS a way. I'm so excited for who I am becoming. I'm growing like bamboo everyday out here. Forcing me to LEAP outside my comfort zone and venture into the unknown. But one thing has remained true. If you truly 'HAVE NO DOUBT' and keep your eyes and mind on the prize the universe WILL provide.

This is only the beginning for me and I'm sure there are more 'growth opportunities' on the way... but I'm ready."

The Real Test Begins

Just when I thought I had life under control, the universe decided to test me again—I lost my only bank card. Now imagine being halfway across the world in South Korea, trying to resolve banking issues with Bank of America. Picture explaining to a customer service rep that you're not making "suspicious transactions in Asia" - you actually ARE in Asia, while your stomach growls loud enough to wake up the entire time zone.

With no access to my funds, I had to make every bit of cash stretch as far as possible. My daily menu? One pack of spicy ramen, a share size bag of Starbursts I got in the airport, and, on a good day, a Korean fried chicken combo. I was basically a college student again, minus the fun parts.

Luckily, the school served lunch. But trying to divide up nine portions of rice between kindergarten boys? Ever seen piranhas in a feeding frenzy? Now imagine those piranhas are four years old, don't speak your language, and have the hand-eye coordination of drunk puppies. There I am, trying to maintain order while Ji-ho is somehow getting rice in his hair, Min-jun is treating his spoon like a catapult, and Sung-min is negotiating rice trades like a Wall Street broker.

The phrase "hangry" takes on a whole new meaning when you're meditating food disputes in Korean kindergarten while surviving on Starbursts and prayer.

And talk about timing. I landed in Korea right as COVID hit. But this wasn't just bad timing - this was comedy-level timing. Instead of jumping into teaching, my first two weeks consisted of sitting in an empty school, making phone calls to confused families who had no idea who this random American was trying to speak to their children.

Picture this: I'm two weeks into being in Korea, still can't work my apartment door code reliably, living on ramen and Starbursts, when suddenly I'm sitting in what feels like divorce court negotiations between the teachers and director.

Director: "This is ridiculous! We're in a difficult situation too!"

Teacher: "Is this reasonable? You're trying to work us like slaves!"

And remember, this is all happening in Korean. To say the air was tense would be an understatement.

Me, sipping water awkwardly: "...should I maybe go make some more phone calls?"

But those phone calls? They were their own special kind of hell. Try to imagine this conversation happening thirty times a day:

"Hi, Mrs. Kim? This is Teacher Nick... um, English teacher? Your son's teacher?"
Confused Korean
"Ji-ho? Can I speak to Ji-ho?"
More confused Korean, shuffling sounds
"Ji-ho! Hi! Are yOu HaViNg A gOoD dAy?!"
"...happy."
"Great! Did you read the red story chapter we sent home?"
"...happy."

The Evolution

Finally, we got back to in-person classes. That's when the real fun started.

Picture this: I'm at the front of my classroom, trying to teach the letter "A" using the textbook's brilliant example of... "ASTRONAUT." Because apparently, that's what you teach Korean kindergarteners as their first English word. Not "apple" or "ant" - straight to space exploration.

Me: "A is for... Astronaut!"
Blank stares
Me: *attempting to mime space walking*
Kids: *still confused*
Me: "You know... space? Moon? NASA?"

And that's when it happened. In the middle of my award-winning performance of zero-gravity floating, two little girls start screaming at each other in rapid-fire Korean. One of them bursts into tears.

There I am, still frozen in my astronaut pose, thinking they're probably arguing about who gets to use the pink crayon or something typical of four-year-olds.

Me: "Okay, let's get back to our friendly neighborhood astronaut..."

Later, my co-teacher pulls me aside: "Do you know what they were fighting about?" "The pink crayon?" "No... Seo-yeon threatened to kill Min-ah and her entire family."

I nearly choked.

Here I was, worried about teaching "ASTRONAUT" to four-year-olds, while actual death threats were being exchanged during my lesson. In kindergarten. Over what, I still have no idea - but somewhere between the kid who silently sat in his own pee and the mini mafia boss making threats, I realized teaching English was going to be the least of my challenges.

And just when the classroom chaos couldn't get any wilder, things at school took another turn. The director decided that with students dropping out due to COVID, we needed to "step up our efforts." This meant:

- More classes
- Weekend work
- Only THREE vacation days a year
- One teacher off at a time maximum

Now picture this: We're having a round table meeting, Korean teachers on one side, foreign teachers on the other, tensions high. I'm sitting there, 3 weeks into being in Korea, still rationing my ramen, and they turn to me:

"Nick? What do you think about all this? This isn't fair right?!"

Like... what am I supposed to say? "UM? I JUST GOT HERE? I NEED MONEY? I DON'T WANNA BE HOMELESS IN KOREA? – Also I'm still trying to figure out how to tell Ji-ho's mom I'm his English teacher!"

The air was thick with passive-aggressive energy. Teachers and director firing heated words back and forth in Korean. Meanwhile, I'm just trying to track who's allowed to go on vacation when, while also figuring out why our textbook thinks "PNEUMONIA" is an appropriate vocabulary word for five-year-olds.

Between the director's demands, the mounting tensions, and the endless phone calls to confused parents, things at the school were becoming more trouble than they were worth. But something else was happening too - that passion for design that had always burned inside me was getting stronger.

Every day I spent teaching "ASTRONAUT" to kindergarteners was a day I wasn't creating, wasn't designing, wasn't building what I knew I was meant to build. The fire inside wouldn't let me ignore it anymore.

That's when I made the call to my grandmother. In the TEFL world, they call what I was about to do a "midnight run" - when a teacher decides they've had enough and makes a swift exit. It's not the most professional move, but sometimes you have to choose yourself.

"Grandma, I don't want to feel like I failed... Coming back earlier than planned feels like giving up."

Her response changed everything. She wasn't concerned about me leaving - she was focused on what came next.

"Just make sure you have a plan when you return," she said. "A lot of places are closed due to lockdown. I don't want you getting into a mental rut."

Still processing this transition, I shared a thought: "Yea, I know... Man, if I could only get a few more clients like my first client who paid me $1500 for a pitch deck, I could really make a living..."

What happened next still gives me chills.

SECONDS after hanging up the phone - I mean literally seconds - my phone lit up with a text. From who? That VERY SAME CLIENT who paid me my first $1500! We hadn't spoken in months, and here he was, reaching out about upcoming projects, wondering if I was available for more work.

He had no idea I was on the complete other side of the earth, dealing with kindergarten mafia bosses and textbooks that thought "XYLO-PHONE" was a good first word. I simply told him I was "out of town" but would absolutely love to reconnect as soon as I returned.

That text wasn't just perfect timing - it was confirmation. Every bizarre moment in Korea had been preparing me for something bigger:

- Those phone calls with confused parents? Perfect training for explaining complex ideas to clients
- Teaching without sharing a language? Invaluable practice for communicating across any barrier
- Managing classroom chaos? Exactly what I needed for juggling multiple client projects
- Reading energy instead of relying on words? The ultimate skill for building a digital business

I was proud of what I'd accomplished. Proud of all those late nights getting TEFL certified while others were out partying. Proud of the hours spent creating curriculum when I could've been watching Netflix. Proud of figuring out how to file the proper paperwork, get approved, find a job, and actually move to a foreign country.

That kind of bravery? That kind of commitment? That doesn't just disappear because things didn't go as planned.

I wasn't leaving Korea because I failed. I was leaving because I'd succeeded in ways I couldn't have imagined. Every challenge - from that first night being locked out, to the subway WiFi quest, to surviving kindergarten death threats - had built something in me that no comfortable job ever could.

What looked like chaos was actually alignment. What felt like setbacks were actually setups. And that burning passion for design? It wasn't just a career path - it was my way forward.

Looking back now, it's wild how it all connected. That last night in Korea, packing up my tiny apartment, staring at my twin sized bed and old coloring pages of astronauts, everything clicked into place.

If I could navigate a foreign subway system without speaking the language, I could definitely build a business where I already spoke the language. If I could teach kindergarteners through a phone, I could handle any client call. If I could adapt to teaching in a foreign country, I could handle any business challenge that came my way.

This wasn't just confidence - it was earned certainty. The kind that only comes from proving yourself in the most challenging circumstances. From being locked out at midnight to quitting my 9-5 design job, from teaching "ASTRONAUT" to four-year-olds to building a digital empire - it all came down to one thing:

When you strip away all your normal tools, when you can't rely on language or cultural references or even basic assumptions, you learn to trust something deeper. You learn to trust yourself.

That client's text wasn't just an opportunity. It was the universe saying: "See? Everything you just went through? It was all preparation for what's next."

Like Simba, I was returning to claim my rightful place. Not as the same person who left - but as someone who had been tested, transformed, and proven in ways that no comfortable life could have created.

Because here's the truth about real transformation: Sometimes you have to leave everything you know to find everything you're capable of becoming.

The Real Lesson

Every challenge you face is preparing you for something bigger. The question isn't "Why is this happening to me?" but "What is this preparing me for?"

When you're stripped of familiar tools, you develop new ones. When you can't rely on words, you master energy. When you're thrown into chaos, you create systems. And when you're tested beyond your limits, you discover they were never real.

The NO DOUBT mindset isn't about avoiding challenges - it's about recognizing them as preparation. Every obstacle is an opportunity.

Every setback is a setup. Every moment of doubt is a chance to prove what you're made of.

Because here's what I learned in Korea: Preparation isn't just about being ready for what you expect. It's about building the confidence to handle what you don't expect.

Your journey might not take you to Korea. But it will take you out of your comfort zone. And when it does, remember this: The challenges aren't trying to break you. They're trying to reveal you.

You're braver than you think. You're stronger than you know. You're ready for more than you imagine.

Now go claim your kingdom.

Let's get it.

Key Takeaways:

- Real growth happens outside your comfort zone
- When stripped of familiar tools, you discover new strengths
- Every challenge is preparation for something bigger
- True confidence is earned through facing uncertainty

Your Turn:

1. Identify your comfort zone's edge
2. Choose one challenge that scares you
3. Document your growth through adversity

4. Turn your setbacks into setups

What's Next: We'll discover how to build a legacy that outlasts our achievements.

PART IV: EXPANSION AND GROWTH

You've awakened. You've broken through. You've built the foundation. Now, it's time to expand. This is where you take the lessons, the strength, and the systems you've developed and use them to create something bigger than yourself.

In these chapters, we'll explore what it means to live the NO DOUBT lifestyle—not just striving for success but for significance. You'll learn how to scale your vision, create impact, and leave a legacy that inspires others to chase their own dreams.

But growth isn't just about reaching new heights; it's about deepening your purpose and aligning your actions with what truly matters. It's about living fully, authentically, and unapologetically.

The journey doesn't end here—it evolves. Because expansion is a lifelong process, and the more you grow, the more you discover how limitless your potential truly is.

Let's rise.

12

Beyond Success: Building Your Legacy

You want to know the moment I realized this was about more than just success?

Two a.m. I'm staring at my crypto account showing a $100K balance. It hits me - this isn't just about me anymore. This is about impact. About creating something that lasts beyond my own success.

Even after losing it all, that realization stuck. Money comes and goes. True legacy is about the lives you touch, the changes you create, the wisdom you pass on.

When my brother passed, it forced me to think about what we leave behind. Success isn't just about personal achievement - it's about creating ripples that continue long after we're gone.

Think about Michael's journey—from gold chains and late nights to building systems and leading teams in Montana. His transformation didn't just change his life. It changed:

- His family's future
- His team's possibilities
- His community's standards
- The next generation's vision of what's possible

That's legacy in action. Not just personal success, but creating a blueprint that others can follow.

But here's what most people get wrong about building legacy:

They think it's about:

- Getting their name on buildings
- Accumulating wealth
- Achieving status
- Being remembered

F' THAT.

Real legacy is about one thing: TRANSFORMATION.

Not just your own transformation. But becoming a force that transforms others.

Let me show you what this really looks like...

The Truth About Legacy

When my brother passed, something hit me harder than the grief: Every unrealized dream dies with you. Every unopened gift gets buried. Every untapped power goes to waste. And that's not just a tragedy for you - it's a theft from everyone your fully-expressed self could have helped.

Think about that.

Think about if my brother Daniel Redd's death had just been an ending. If I had let that pain break me instead of build me. Think about every person reading this book right now who wouldn't have woken up to their own power.

That's why legacy isn't optional. It's a fucking responsibility.

The Three Dimensions Of Legacy

Personal Legacy: The Lives You Touch

This isn't about numbers. It's about depth.

- Every client you transform
- Every person you inspire
- Every soul you wake up
- Every life you change

When I look at Michael crushing it in Montana, living his dream, I don't just see his success. I see:

- His future kids growing up with a father who showed them what's possible
- His clients building their dreams because he found the courage to build his
- Every person who sees his story and realizes they can change too

That's a sacred geometrical impact. That's legacy in motion.

Systemic Legacy: The Structures You Build

This is where it gets interesting. This is about building:

- Systems that empower others
- Frameworks that transfer wisdom
- Platforms that amplify impact
- Methods that multiply transformation

Remember the NO DOUBT METHOD? It's not just a system. It's a transformation machine that will be changing lives long after we're gone.

Cultural Legacy: The Shifts You Create
This is the deepest level. This is about changing:

- How people think
- What people believe is possible
- What becomes normal

- What gets passed on

Every time someone chooses:

- Power over fear
- Growth over comfort
- Truth over safety
- Impact over approval

They're not just changing their life. They're shifting the cultural DNA. They're upgrading what's possible for everyone who comes after.

The Legacy Code

Want to know how to build something that lasts?

Here's the real code:

Document Everything
- Your breakthroughs
- Your systems
- Your insights
- Your transformations

Not for your ego. For those who come next.

Transfer Everything
- Your knowledge
- Your wisdom
- Your methods

- Your power

Make yourself replaceable. That's how you become eternal.

Build Beyond Yourself
- Create leaders
- Empower others
- Share the keys
- Light the way

The Power Of Legacy In Action

Here's what most people never understand about building legacy:

You don't wait until you're "successful enough." You don't wait until you're "ready." You don't wait until you're "qualified."

You start right now. Today.

The Daily Legacy Protocol

Morning Power Hour (4:30 AM - 5:30 AM)

Ask yourself:

- Who needs my light today?
- What wisdom am I hiding?
- What impact am I playing small with?

• How can I serve at a higher level?

Then transform those answers into action.

Creation Time (5:30 AM - 9:30 AM)

This isn't just about making things. This is about creating:

- Systems that liberate people
- Content that transforms lives
- Tools that transfer power
- Methods that multiply impact

Remember: Every time you solve a problem, document the solution. That's not just efficiency - that's legacy in motion.

Impact Hours (10:00 AM - 3:00 PM)
This is where transformation happens:

- Teach everything you know
- Share every solution you find
- Light every path you've walked
- Open every door you've unlocked

Because here's the absolute truth about legacy:

- Information kept secret dies with you.
- Knowledge hoarded helps no one.
- Power unexpressed serves nothing.

- Wisdom unshared changes nothing.
- The Multiplication Effect

Want to see real power in action?

Watch what happens when one person fully steps into their potential:

- Their family starts dreaming bigger
- Their friends begin questioning limits
- Their community sees new possibilities
- Their impact creates ripples they'll never even see

This isn't theory. I've watched it happen.

When I saw Michael transform from lost to living his purpose, it wasn't just his life that changed. His courage sparked something in others. His clients started taking bigger risks. His work began inspiring people he'd never meet. His story became proof of what's possible.

That's the multiplication effect in action.

Building Legacy Systems

Here's where most people miss the opportunity for lasting impact. They try to:

- Do everything themselves
- Keep all the knowledge

- Control every outcome
- Be the hero of every story

But true legacy builders? They think differently. They build:

1. **Knowledge Transfer Systems**

- Document every process
- Record every insight
- Map every solution
- Make wisdom accessible

1. **Power Multiplication Systems**

- Train other leaders
- Create clear frameworks
- Build repeatable methods
- Enable others to teach

1. **Impact Scaling Systems**

- Design for expansion
- Plan for succession
- Build beyond yourself
- Create self-sustaining momentum

The Ultimate Question

Every morning when you wake up, ask yourself:

"If everything I built disappeared tomorrow, what would remain in the people I've touched?"

Because that's the real measure of legacy:

- Not your bank account, but the abundance you've created in others
- Not your achievements, but the barriers you've broken for others
- Not your success, but the dreams you've awakened in others
- Not your power, but the potential you've unleashed in others

Turning Legacy Into Reality

Here's your implementation blueprint:

The Knowledge Vault
Every week, capture:

- One major lesson learned
- One system refined
- One insight gained
- One transformation created

Document it. Share it. Build the vault.

The Power Transfer
Every month, ensure:

- Someone learns your methods
- Someone gains your skills

- Someone adopts your systems
- Someone carries your torch

The Impact Accelerator
Every quarter, check:

- Are others teaching your methods?
- Is your impact multiplying?
- Are systems running without you?
- Is transformation happening automatically?

Remember this:

True power isn't in what you build. It's in what continues building after you're gone.

Your legacy starts now.

Let's build something eternal.

Key Takeaways:

- Real legacy is about transformation, not recognition
- Your impact multiplies through the lives you touch
- True power lives in what continues building after you're gone
- Legacy isn't about waiting - it's about starting now

Your Turn:

1. Define your legacy vision

2. Build your knowledge transfer system
3. Document one breakthrough this week
4. Start your power multiplication chain

What's Next: We'll explore how to turn these principles into your daily lifestyle.

13

The NO DOUBT Lifestyle

Now Wake Up.

No one is coming to save you. No one is going to hand you your dreams. No one is going to unleash your power for you.

That future you keep dreaming about?

It's not going to magically appear while you're scrolling on your phone, waiting for *"someday."*

This isn't about motivation.
This isn't about inspiration.
This is about the **raw fucking truth** of what it takes.

The Battle With Doubt

Every morning when I hit that floor for push-up number one, doubt is right there waiting:

Telling me to quit.
Telling me to take it easy.
Telling me to go back to bed.
Telling me I've done enough.

But here's the truth:

Doubt doesn't go away. You just have to become stronger than it.

Every. Single. Day.

Stop Waiting

I see people walking around half-alive, waiting:

Waiting for the perfect moment
Waiting for permission
Waiting for someone to believe in them
Waiting for life to get easier

Stop waiting.

That design empire you want to build? That impact you want to make? That power you want to unleash?
It's all possible. But you have to will it into existence.

Every. Single. Damn. Day.

Not just when you feel motivated. Not just when it's convenient. Not just when others believe in you.

I had to will myself out of my limiting 9-5. Will myself through 1,000 push-ups. Will myself past every "no." Will myself beyond every doubt.

No one did it for me. No one's going to do it for you.

The world doesn't care about your potential. It doesn't care about your excuses or how hard your life is. It cares about what you create. What you build. What you become.

The Daily Battle

You're going to face doubt every day.

It'll be there when your alarm goes off. When you're about to take that risk. When you're staring at a blank screen. When you're standing at the edge of your comfort zone.

Good.

Let it come.

Because here's what most people never understand: Doubt isn't your enemy. It's your compass. It points directly at what you need to do next.

When I stood in that cubicle, staring at another car ad, doubt screamed at me to stay safe. To keep the steady paycheck. To stop dreaming so big.

Instead of running from that feeling, I used it as fuel.

Every time doubt says "you can't" - that's exactly where you need to go.
Every time it whispers "play small" - that's exactly when you need to expand.
Every time it begs "stay safe" - that's exactly when you need to leap.

This isn't about being fearless. This is about being unstoppable.

Right now, doubt is probably telling you this isn't possible for you. That this message isn't meant for you. That your dreams are too big. That you should stay realistic.

Listen closely to that voice. Because that's your roadmap. That's your blueprint. That's exactly what you need to prove wrong.

Most people will spend their whole lives running from doubt.

Not you. Not anymore.

From this moment forward, you run straight at it.

When it tells you "that client is out of your league" - you send the proposal.
When it says "you're not ready for that project" - you take it on.

When it whispers "who do you think you are" - you show it exactly who you've become.

I'm not talking about blind confidence. I'm talking about raw determination.

The kind that got me through push-up 999 when my arms were shaking. The kind that kept me going when my crypto account hit zero. The kind that turned being locked out in Korea into proof that nothing could stop me.

This isn't about talent. This isn't about luck. This isn't about perfect timing.
This is about waking up every single day and deciding that doubt doesn't get to win today.

The Real Power

When you live like this - really live like this - something shifts.
Not overnight. Not in some magical transformation. But in the daily decision to be unstoppable.

Here's what happens when you make this your reality:

You start moving different. Not because you're trying to. Because doubt doesn't own you anymore.

That design you were scared to show? You ship it. That price you were afraid to charge? You name it. That dream that felt too big? You claim it.

Every day becomes a battle between who you were and who you're becoming.

And let me tell you something: That battle never ends. It never gets easier. You just get stronger.

I still feel doubt every morning. Still hear that voice saying "take it easy." Still feel that pull toward comfort.

But now I know: That's not doubt trying to protect me. That's doubt trying to stop me. That's doubt trying to keep me small.

And I refuse to stay small.

Every time you choose power over comfort, every time you choose growth over safety, every time you choose truth over fear, you become more of who you're meant to be.

This is your life. This is your power. This is your time.

What are you going to do about it?

Some people will tell you it gets easier. They're lying.

What actually happens is this: **You get harder to kill. You get harder to stop. You get harder to doubt.**

The Ultimate Choice

Every morning when that alarm goes off, you have a choice: Be comfortable or be unstoppable. Stay safe or become powerful. Hide from doubt or use it as fuel.

I'm not talking about some grand moment of courage. I'm talking about the small decisions that build an unstoppable life:

When you're tired but you ship the work anyway.
When you're scared but you hit send anyway.
When you're uncertain but you make the call anyway.
When doubt is screaming but you keep moving anyway.

That's how you build power. Not in one moment. Not in one victory. But in the constant decision to be unstoppable.

Stop waiting. Start becoming.

Your power doesn't need permission. It just needs your decision.

What's it going to be?

The time for doubt is over. The time for waiting is done. The time for hiding has passed.

This is your moment.

Now rise.

KEY TAKEAWAYS

- Doubt doesn't go away - you become stronger than it.
- Your power isn't waiting for confidence - it's waiting for decision.
- Every great achievement started with someone refusing to stay small.
- Your time isn't coming - it's now.

YOUR TURN

1. Face your biggest doubt today.
2. Make the decision that scares you.
3. Take action before you feel ready.
4. Choose power over comfort.

WHAT'S NEXT

Time for REAL TALK - No more excuses.

14

Conclusion: No More Excuses

"(S)HE THAT IS GOOD FOR MAKING EXCUSES IS SEL-DOM GOOD FOR ANYTHING ELSE." — *BENJAMIN FRANKLIN*

Let me be clear: Reading this book isn't enough. Knowledge without action is just entertainment. And you didn't come here to be entertained - you came here to be transformed.

So let's get real. Right now, you're at a crossroads:

Path 1: Close this book, feel inspired for a few days, then slide back into old patterns. Keep living with that voice of doubt. Keep playing small. Keep waiting for "someday."

Path 2: Take everything you've learned and turn it into action. Start your transformation TODAY. Not tomorrow. Not next week. Not when you "feel ready." NOW.

The choice is yours. But let me tell you something: That fire you feel in your chest while reading these words? That's not excitement. That's recognition. Your soul recognizing its own power.

Your NO DOUBT Blueprint

Here's exactly what to do next:

1. **Morning Revolution**

- Wake up one hour earlier than usual
- Start with the 2-Minute Emotional Release Technique
- Do something that scares you before breakfast

1. **Daily Deep Work**

- Block 90 minutes for focused creation
- No distractions, no exceptions
- Build something that matters

1. **Evening Audit**

- Review your actions against your values
- Document your wins, however small
- Plan tomorrow's breakthrough

1. **Weekly Integration**

- Connect with growth-minded people
- Study something that stretches you

• Create value for others

The Final Push

Remember when I lost $100K in crypto? When I was locked out of my apartment in Korea? When I got the call about my brother?

Each moment could have broken me. Instead, they built me. Because I chose to use them as fuel.

You've got your own moments. Your own pain. Your own challenges. The question isn't whether you have what it takes - you wouldn't have read this far if you didn't.

The question is: What are you going to do with it?

Your Turn

Right now, take out your phone. Set a reminder for 4:30 AM tomorrow. When it goes off, you have a choice to make:

Stay comfortable in your doubt, or rise with NO DOUBT.

Keep making excuses, or start making history.

Keep waiting for permission, or start giving yourself authority.

The Ultimate Truth

You don't need:

- Perfect circumstances
- Complete clarity
- Everyone's approval
- More time

You just need to decide: Is this the moment you finally unleash your power?

Look, I'm not special. Those 1,000 push-ups I used to do every morning? I outgrew them. Not because they got easier, but because growth means evolution. Now I mix up my workouts, challenge my body in new ways, keep pushing boundaries. That's what this journey is about - constant evolution, never settling, always pushing forward.

And that's what I want for you. Not to copy my path, but to create your own. To push past your comfort zone, to break through your limitations, to become the person you're meant to be.

The Real Talk: No More Excuses

I already know what some of you might be thinking:

"Honestly, I'm just scared I won't make it..."

Listen - fear is normal. But you know what's scarier than failing? Looking back at your life in 40 years knowing you never even tried. The pain of regret lasts way longer than the pain of failure.

"It's just so hard though..."

Of course it's hard. That's why most people won't do it. But you're not most people - you wouldn't have read this far if you were. Hard is what makes it worth doing. Hard is what makes it yours.

"I'm just so lost though..."

Being lost is a starting point, not a life sentence. You think I had it all figured out in my mom's basement? In Korea? After losing everything in crypto? Hell no. But you don't need to see the whole staircase to take the first step. Start walking. The path reveals itself to those who move.

Here's the truth, and I need you to hear this: You already have everything you need. The power, the potential, the possibility - it's all there. The only thing standing between you and your dreams is that voice of doubt in your head.

Look, I get it. These fears feel real because they are real. But here's what's also real: Your power. Your potential. Your ability to transform everything about your life the moment you decide to stop doubting and start doing.

Just like that person who reached out before this book even existed, there are people out there right now waiting for what only you can create. They're waiting for your story, your art, your business, your impact.

Don't make them wait any longer.

The world needs your gifts. It needs your voice. It needs your courage. It needs your light.

The only question is: Are you ready to prove to yourself what's possible when you HAVE NO DOUBT?

The world is waiting. Your destiny is waiting. Your greatness is waiting.

Stop making them wait.

Get up. Get moving. Get after it.

Your time isn't coming - it's here.

Let's get it.

The power is in you. It always has been. Now go prove it to yourself.

Appendix

TOOLS FOR TRANSFORMATION

---

1. THE NO DOUBT METHOD *(Chapter 1)*

- **Step 1:** Locate Your Limitation
- **Step 2:** Create Your System
- **Step 3:** Take Daily Action
- **Step 4:** Track Progress
- **Step 5:** Scale Impact

2. THE EMOTIONAL RELEASE TECHNIQUE *(Chapter 2)*

- **Two-Minute Timer**
- **Location Protocol**
- **Energy Redirection**
- **Integration Practice**

3. DEEP WORK PROTOCOL *(Chapter 5)*

- **Morning Power Block:** 4:30–7:30 AM
- **Focus Sessions:** 90-minute blocks
- **Environment Design**
- **Progress Tracking**

4. THE CREATOR'S CODE *(Chapter 9)*

- **Level 1:** Execution
- **Level 2:** Solution

- **Level 3:** Transformation

5. LEGACY BUILDING SYSTEM *(Chapter 12)*

- **Knowledge Transfer**
- **Impact Multiplication**
- **Culture Creation**
- **Sustainability Check**

RECOMMENDED READING

Mindset & Philosophy

- *The Alchemist* by Paulo Coelho
- *As a Man Thinketh* by James Allen
- *Meditations* by Marcus Aurelius
- *The Power of NOW* by Eckhart Tolle
- *The Four Agreements* by Don Miguel Ruiz

Success & Strategy

- *Think and Grow Rich* by Napoleon Hill
- *The 10X Rule* by Grant Cardone
- *Deep Work* by Cal Newport
- *The Slight Edge* by Jeff Olson
- *Unlimited Power* by Tony Robbins

Growth & Psychology

- *Psycho-Cybernetics* by Maxwell Maltz
- *Mindset* by Carol S. Dweck
- *Influence* by Robert B. Cialdini
- *The Obstacle is the Way* by Ryan Holiday
- *Creative Inc.* by Amy Wallace and Edwin Catmull

ESSENTIAL TOOLS & SOFTWARE

Project Management

- *Monday.com* – Team and project organization
- *Slack* – Team communication and collaboration
- *Google Drive* – Document management and sharing

Design & Creation

- *Photoshop* – Professional design (optional)
- *Canva* – Accessible design for everyone

Productivity

- *Notes* – Time tracking and daily planning

CONNECT & LEARN MORE

The Power of NO DOUBT™
www.thepowerofnodoubt.com

NO DOUBT Studios
www.nodoubtstudios.com

NO DOUBT APPAREL™
www.ndapparelonlinestore.com

Social Media
@nickdavidnodoubt – on everything

Acknowledgments

To my grandparents,

Dr. Charles & Martha Warfield, thank you for paving the way for my future. Your continuous investment in my growth—both personally and spiritually—has shaped the man I am today. You instilled in me the importance of education, faith, and perseverance, values that have become the bedrock of my journey. Your wisdom, resilience, and legacy inspire me daily to reach higher, do better, and never stop growing. I am forever grateful for the roots you planted and the path you cleared so that I could walk confidently toward my purpose.

To my mother,
Your boundless love has been my anchor through every storm. You've taught me the power of compassion, resilience, and unwavering belief in others. But most importantly, you taught me faith in God—how to trust, pray, and lean into His guidance through life's challenges. Your encouragement and spiritual foundation have been the light that keeps me grounded and focused.

To my father,

Your relentlessness in pursuing excellence and your commitment to hard work have been the foundation of my drive. You've shown me the importance of discipline, determination, and pushing beyond limits to achieve greatness. Your example has taught me that success is earned through grit and perseverance.

With all my love and gratitude,

Nicholas David Warfield

About the Author

Nicholas David is a designer, entrepreneur, and founder of NO DOUBT, a global movement dedicated to helping people eliminate self-doubt and unlock their true potential. His journey from small-town designer to global entrepreneur has been anything but conventional. After losing his brother—a moment that split his life into "before" and "after"—he transformed tragedy into rocket fuel for growth, building NO DOUBT from a mindset into a movement.

From teaching English in South Korea during a global pandemic to building a six-figure design studio, from losing (and rebuilding) a financial portfolio to helping others break free from their own limitations, Nicholas has turned every setback into a setup for something greater. Through NO DOUBT Nation, NO DOUBT Studios, and NO DOUBT APPAREL™, he's created a multi-faceted empire dedicated to one mission: showing others what's possible when they eliminate self-doubt.

His unique approach combines raw authenticity with practical systems, helping creators, entrepreneurs, and dreamers turn their gifts into global impact. While others talk about motivation, Nick focuses on transformation—providing battle-tested strategies that create real, lasting change.

His work extends beyond business success. He's helped countless individuals break through their limitations, build thriving enterprises, and discover their true potential. His message of unwavering self-belief has inspired thousands across social media and beyond, creating a community of people committed to becoming unstoppable.

This debut book marks the beginning of a powerful series dedicated to showing what's possible when you eliminate doubt, embrace your full potential, and live with NO DOUBT.

THE NEXT STEP

If you're feeling that fire right now - that urge to take everything you've learned and push it even further - I want to help you make it happen.

Just You, Me and Your NO DOUBT Dreams

If you're serious about having a personal guide through this journey - someone who's walked this path and can help you navigate your own - then let's talk. Through one-on-one coaching, I'll be right there with you, helping you:

- Break through your specific barriers
- Build your personal roadmap
- Create real, lasting transformation
- Turn your dreams into reality

This isn't for everyone. It's for people who are ready to put in the work, who want someone in their corner pushing them to levels they never thought possible.

Want to Move at Your Own Pace?

I get it. Maybe you're not ready for that level of intensity yet. Head over to powerofnodoubt.com - we've created a complete program that lets you dive deeper into these principles and implement them at your own speed. Same transformation, self-guided path.

Speaking Truth to Power

And listen - if you're running a company, organization, or event and you want to bring this energy to your people, let's make it happen. I'll come in and light that fire, wake people up to their own power, and show them what's possible when they HAVE NO DOUBT.

Ready to take this journey further?

Visit powerofnodoubt.com or hit me up at info@powerofnodoubt.com

Remember: This book isn't the end. It's your invitation to something bigger.

Let's get it.

The next chapter of your story starts now. You ready?

www.ingramcontent.com/pod-product-compliance
Lightning Source LLC
Chambersburg PA
CBHW021843130726
47989CB00009B/3069